Active Learning for Recommender Systems

Active Learning for Recommender Systems

A thesis submitted for the degree of

Doctor of Natural Science (Dr. rer. nat.)

by

Rasoul Karimi

Department of Computer Science

Information Systems and Machine Learning Lab (ISMLL)

University of Hildesheim, Germany

Supervisor: Prof. Dr. Dr. Lars Schmidt-Thieme

Winter 2014

Bibliografische Information der Deutschen Nationalbibliothek
Die Deutsche Nationalbibliothek verzeichnet diese Publikation in der Deutschen Nationalbibliographie; detaillierte bibliographische Daten sind im Internet über http://dnb.d-nb.de abrufbar.
1. Aufl. - Göttingen: Cuvillier, 2014
Zugl.: Hildesheim, Univ., Diss., 2014

Nonnenstieg 8, 37075 Göttingen
Telefon: 0551-54724-0
Telefax: 0551-54724-21
www.cuvillier.de

1. Auflage 2014
Gedruckt auf umweltfreundlichem, säurefreiem Papier aus nachhaltiger Forstwirtschaft.

ISBN 978-3-95404-692-8
eISBN 978-3-7369-4692-7

To my family

Acknowledgements

My sincere gratitude goes first to Prof. Dr. Dr. Lars Schmidt-Thieme, my supervisor in the last five years. He provided me the opportunity of studying in his group and growing up as a research scientist. Besides my supervisor, I would like to thank Prof. Dr. Alexandros Nanopoulos, my co-supervisor in the first three years of my PhD studies. His advice on both research as well as on the REMIX project have been priceless. I would also like to thank all current and former members of the Information Systems and Machine Learning Lab (ISMLL) at the University of Hildesheim, in particular my co-authors, Christoph Freudenthaler and Martin Wistuba for their fruitful research cooperation. In the end, I would like to show my gratitude to late Prof. Caro Lucas, my former supervisor in the University of Tehran. God rest his soul in peace.

Abstract

Nowadays we are living in an era that is overloaded with information. Decision-making in this environment can sometimes become a nightmare. There are too many choices and we simply cannot explore them all. Therefore, it would be really helpful to have a system to help us to find the right choice. Such systems, which learn user preferences and provide personalized recommendations to them are called *Recommender Systems*.

Evidently, the performance of recommender systems depends on the amount of information that users provide regarding items, most often in the form of ratings. This problem is amplified for new users because they have not provided any rating, which impacts negatively on the quality of generated recommendations. This problem is called *new user problem* or *cold-start problem*. A simple and effective way to overcome this problem, is by posing queries to new users so that they express their preferences about selected items, e.g. by rating them. Nevertheless, the selection of items must take into consideration that users are not willing to answer a lot of such queries. To address this problem, *active learning* methods have been proposed to acquire the most informative ratings, i.e ratings from users that will help most in determining their interests.

The aim of this thesis is to take inspiration from the literature of active learning for machine learning and develop new methods for the new user problem in recommender systems. In the recommender system context, new users play the role of the Oracle and provide labels (ratings) to the queries (items). In this approach, we will take into consideration that although there are no data for new users, but there is abundant data for existing users. Such additional data can help us to develop scalable and accurate active learning methods for the new user problem in recommender systems.

The thesis consists of two parts. In the first part, to be consistent with the settings of active learning in machine learning and the related works on the new user problem in recommender system, it is assumed that the new user is always able to rate the queried items. Next, this constraint is relaxed and new users are allowed not to rate the items.

Most of the developed active learning methods exploit the characteristics matrix factorization because nevertheless, recent research (especially as has been demonstrated during the Netflix challenge) indicates that matrix factorization is a superior prediction model for recommender systems compared to other approaches.

Contents

List of Figures

List of Tables

Notation

This thesis will adhere to the following notational conventions:

U	set of users
u	user u
I	set of items
i	item i
R	set of ratings
r	actual rating
$\hat{r}$	predicted rating
$.$	missing rating
R^+	set of ratings including the missing rating
$\mathcal{D}$	a dataset
q	q-query
$\mathcal{D}^{\text{train}}$	the training dataset
$\mathcal{D}^{\text{test}}$	the test dataset
$\mathcal{D}^{\text{pool}}$	the pool dataset
$\mathcal{D}^{query}$	the dataset containing the new user's answers to the queries
$\mathcal{D}_u$	a subset of $\mathcal{D}^{\text{train}}$, containing the ratings of user u
$\mathcal{D}_i$	a subset of $\mathcal{D}^{\text{train}}$ containing the ratings of item i
t	a node in decision trees
$\mathcal{D}^t$	a subset of $\mathcal{D}^{\text{train}}$ containing the ratings of users, associated with the node t
N	maximum number of queries
(u, i, r)	a triple containing the rating r of user u to item i
$\bar{R}_i$	the predicted rating for item i using the item average method
ℓ	a loss function
F	a learning algorithm
k	the number of latent features
μ	global average
b_u	the user bias of user u
b_i	the item bias of item i
W	a matrix containing user features in matrix factorization
H	a matrix containing item features in matrix factorization
w_u	the features of user u in the matrix factorization
h_i	the features of item i in matrix factorization

w_{uf}	The f-th latent feature of user u
h_{if}	The fth latent feature of item i
λ	the regularization factor
L	maximum number of training epochs in matrix factorization
ϵ	the convergence error in matrix factorization
θ	aspect model parameters
z	aspect model class

Abbreviation

This thesis will use to the following abbreviations:

MF	Matrix Factorization
AM	Aspect Model
MAE	Mean Absolute Error
RMSE	Root Mean Square Deviation
FDT	Factorized Decision Trees
MPS	Most Popular Sampling
REMIX	RFID-Enhanced Museum for Interactive Experience
PDA	Personal Digital Assistant
SGD	Stochastic Gradient Descent
EM	Expected Maximization
RFID	Radio-frequency identification
MPAM	Most Popular for Aspect Model
MPLS	Most Popular in Latent Space
LAL	Learning Active Learning

Chapter 1

Introduction

Nowadays we are living in an era that is overloaded with information. For example, if you enter the word "book" as the keyword for a Google search, you will get about 1,500,000,000 hits! Decision-making in this environment can sometimes become a nightmare. There are too many choices and we simply cannot explore them all. Therefore, it would be really helpful to have a system to help us to find the right choice. Such a system can help us only if it knows what we like and what we do not like. Then, the system can filter irrelevant choices and recommend options that are likely to be interesting for us. Such systems, which learn user preferences and provide personalized recommendations to them are called *Recommender Systems* (Adomavicius & Tuzhilin, 2005; Goldberg *et al.*, 1992; Konstan *et al.*, 1997a).

Today all major web companies are equipped with recommender systems. The recommended item can be anything. To name just a few examples: a book in Amazon, a movie in Netflix, a friend on Facebook, and so on. Table 1.1 summarizes the most important recommender systems in different areas. Recommender systems can also be used for physical environments, such as museums. Visitors to physical museums are often overwhelmed by the vast amount of information available in the space they are exploring, making it difficult for them to select the content that is likely to be interesting to them personally. Recommender systems can recommend specific exhibits that are likely to be interesting to individual visitors (Karimi *et al.*, 2011d).

Recommendation algorithms fall into two main categories: content-based and collaborative filtering (Adomavicius & Tuzhilin, 2005). In the content-based approach, there is a set of attributes for each item. Items that have similar attributes to those that have been liked by the target user are recommended to them. For example, if a user likes a book from an author, another book from the same author is recommended to that user because both books have the same attributes. The main drawback of content-based recommendation is that it requires complete profiles for items (Resnick & Varian, 1997). On the other hand, collaborative filtering does not need such profiles. It predicts the interests of users by reusing taste information from similar users (Burke, 2002a; Konstan *et al.*, 1997a). Also, there are some methods that combine content-

Table 1.1: Examples of recommender systems and their applications

Company	**Category**	**Recommended Item**
Amazon, eBay, Netflix	e-Commerce	Product
Facebook, LinkedIn	Social Network	Friend, Group
YouTube	Social Network	Video Clip
CNN, Routers	News Agency	News, Article
TiVo	Public media channel	TV Channel
Pandaro	Public media channel	Radio Channel
Yahoo! Answer	Q & A Community	Questions
Delicious	Social bookmarking	Web page
Bibsonomy	Social bookmarking	Tags

based and collaborative filtering and call it *hybrid* recommendation algorithms (Burke, 2002b; Pennock *et al.*, 2000; Schein *et al.*, 2002).

The collaborative filtering method falls into two categories: memory-based algorithms and model-based algorithms. In memory-based techniques, the value of the unknown rating is computed as an aggregate of the ratings of some other (usually, the N most similar) users for the same item (Konstan *et al.*, 1997a). Model-based collaborative techniques provide recommendations by estimating parameters of statistical models for user ratings. Nevertheless, recent research (especially as has been demonstrated during the Netflix challenge[1]) indicates that Matrix Factorization (MF) (Koren *et al.*, 2009) is a superior predictive model compared to other approaches (Koren *et al.*, 2009).

1.1 Motivation

Evidently, the performance of collaborative filtering depends on the amount of information that users provide regarding items, most often in the form of ratings. This problem is amplified for new users because they have not provided any rating, which impacts negatively on the quality of generated recommendations. This problem is called *new user problem* or *cold-start problem*. Different approaches can be taken to deal with the cold-start problem. We can switch to content-based algorithms until enough ratings are given by new users. However, this is not possible if items do not have complete attributes. Another possibility is to use non-personalized methods, such as most popular. But such methods do not perform well and it is risky to use them for new users. Note that new users of a recommender system are sensitive, they leave the system if they get a bad first impression and go to competitor systems. Needless to say, new users are vital for the revenue of companies.

A simple and effective way to overcome this problem, is by posing queries to new users so that they express their preferences about selected items, e.g. by rating them.

[1] www.netflixprize.com

Nevertheless, the selection of items must take into consideration that users are not willing to answer a lot of such queries. To address this problem, *active learning* methods have been proposed to acquire the most informative ratings, i.e ratings from users that will help most in determining their interests (Harpale & Yang, 2008; Jin & Si, 2004). In this thesis, we will study the application of active learning for the cold-start problem in recommender systems.

1.2 Contribution

The aim of this thesis is to take inspiration from the literature of active learning for machine learning and develop new methods for the new user problem in recommender systems. The thesis consists of two parts. In the first part, to be consistent with the settings of active learning in machine learning and the related works on the new user problem in recommender system, it is assumed that the new user is always able to rate the queried items. Next, this constraint is relaxed and new users are allowed not to rate the items. Specifically, our contributions are as follows:

- **Formal Definition of Active Learning for Recommender Systems.** We formalize the problem of active learning for recommender systems. To the best of our knowledge, this is the first formal definition of active learning for recommender systems.
- **Active Learning for Aspect Model.** We develop a new active learning method for the aspect model (Hofmann, 2003; Hofmann & Puzicha, 1999). It takes into account the learning algorithm of the aspect model. While this method competes in terms of accuracy with a complicated Bayesian method, it is in the order of magnitude faster than it. Moreover, we compare the aspect model to matrix factorization (Koren, 2008) from the perspective of active learning and show that matrix factorization is more accurate and faster than the aspect model.
- **Active Learning for Matrix Factorization.** We develop five active learning algorithms for the cold-start problem based on matrix factorization. Most of these methods capitalize explicitly on the characteristics of matrix factorization, such as the learning algorithm and similarity in the latent space.
- **Factorized Decision Trees (FDT).** FDT combines the power of matrix factorization with the easy-to-understand structure of decision trees to build adaptive questionnaires. Furthermore, we propose a sampling method to speed up the tree construction algorithm. It is called Most Popular Sampling (MPS).
- **Learning Active Learning** We introduce a new approach for active learning in recommender systems that is called *learning active learning*. The main idea is to consider past users as (artificial) new users in order to learn the right queries to be asked to new users for active-learning purposes.

- **Active Learning for Museum Recommender Systems** We discuss how active learning can be used for recommender systems in museums. As a museum recommender system, we take our own project called RFID-Enhanced Museum for Interactive Experience (REMIX) (Karimi *et al.*, 2011d).
- **Empirical Evaluation and Analysis.** All algorithms proposed in this thesis are thoroughly evaluated on the basis of several real-life datasets and compared to state-of-the-art algorithms.

After mentioning the contributions, we would like to clarify what is not covered in this thesis. The cold-start problem has three meanings: new user, new item and new system. New system means a system that has just been inaugurated, so there are no ratings from any user for any item. Active learning has been applied for the new system problem (Boutilier *et al.*, 2003; Rish & Tesauro, 2008; Rubens & Sugiyama, 2007; Sutherland *et al.*, 2013), the new item problem (Deodhar *et al.*, 2009; Huang, 2007; Park & Chu, 2009). Also, some works combine the new system and new user problem in the sense that they suppose when new users enter the recommender system, there are not yet many active users because the system has not been running for a very long time (Elahi *et al.*, 2012, 2013, 2014). In this thesis, we address only the new user problem, assuming that there are already enough active users in the system. It should be mentioned that in general new user and new item problems are symmetric. However, we will not evaluate the developed methods for the new item problem.

In this thesis, we address the new user problem by posing queries to new users in order to get ratings from them. There are other approaches to deal with this problem that are not the concern of this thesis:

- **Implicit Feedback.** (Zhang *et al.*, 2009; Zigoris, 2006) leverage implicit feedback, such as search keywords or user clicks to learn new user preferences.
- **Content-based recommendation** (Gantner *et al.*, 2010; Gunawardana & Meek, 2008) combine content-based attributes with collaborative filtering.
- **Demographic information.** (Safoury & Salah, 2013) use demographic information on new users.

1.3 Published Work

Most of the work reported in this thesis has already been published at peer-reviewed international conferences:

- Rasoul Karimi, Martin Wistuba, Alexandros Nanopoulos, Lars Schmidt-Thieme (2013): Factorized Decision Trees for Active Learning in Recommender Systems, in Proceedings of the IEEE International Conference on Tools with Artificial Intelligence (ICTAI), Washington D.C, USA.

- Rasoul Karimi, Christoph Freudenthaler, Alexandros Nanopoulos, Lars Schmidt-Thieme (2013): Towards Optimal Active Learning for Matrix Factorization in Recommender Systems, in Workshop on Knowledge Discovery, Data Mining and Machine Learning (KDML-2013), Bamberg, Germany*(resubmission)*
- Rasoul Karimi, Christoph Freudenthaler, Alexandros Nanopoulos, Lars Schmidt-Thieme (2012): Exploiting the Characteristics of Matrix Factorization for Active Learning in Recommender Systems, in Doctoral Symposium of the 6th Annual ACM Conference on Recommender Systems (RecSys), Dublin, Irelan, pp. 317-320
- Rasoul Karimi, Christoph Freudenthaler, Alexandros Nanopoulos, Lars Schmidt-Thieme (2011): Towards Optimal Active Learning for Matrix Factorization in Recommender Systems, in 23th IEEE International Conference on Tools With Artificial Intelligence (ICTAI), Florida, USA.
- Rasoul Karimi, Christoph Freudenthaler, Alexandros Nanopoulos, Lars Schmidt-Thieme (2011): Non-myopic Active Learning for Recommender Systems based on Matrix Factorization, in 12th IEEE International Conference on Information Reuse and Integration (IRI), Las Vegas, USA.
- Rasoul Karimi, Christoph Freudenthaler, Alexandros Nanopoulos, Lars Schmidt-Thieme (2011): Active Learning for Aspect Model in Recommender Systems, in IEEE Symposium on Computational Intelligence and Data Mining (CIDM).
- Rasoul Karimi, Alexandros Nanopoulos, Lars Schmidt-Thieme (2011): RFID-Enhanced Museum for Interactive Experience, in MultiMedia for Cultural Heritage (MM4CH), Modena, Italy

1.4 Chapter Overview

Besides the introduction, this thesis is organized as follows:

- In chapter 2 we formalize the problem of active learning for recommender systems. We introduce notations, which will be used in the rest of the thesis. Furthermore, we describe datasets and the evaluation protocol.
- In chapter 3, we explain the background techniques that are needed to understand this thesis. This consists of two sections: in the first section, different aspects of active learning are discussed and in the second section, the state-of-the-art recommendation methods are illustrated.
- Related work is reviewed in chapter 4. First, the related work on active learning is reviewed, especially those which have influenced cold-start recommendation. Then the related work on active learning for the new user problem in recommender systems is reviewed.

- In chapter 5 we develop an active learning method for the aspect model. It takes into account the learning algorithm of the aspect model, which results in selecting the most popular items. Moreover, we compare the aspect model with matrix factorization taking into account two factors: time and accuracy. The aspect model uses the Expected Maximization learning algorithm and matrix factorization is based on stochastic gradient descent. Although both models have the same time complexity, the results show that matrix factorization is faster because the stochastic gradient descent converges faster. Matrix factorization is also more accurate. This finding is consistent with other reports that matrix factorization performs well in recommender systems, especially after the Netflix prize.

- In chapter 6, by being inspired from the literature of active learning for machine learning, we introduce four active learning criteria for MF. Two methods are based on uncertainty. The third method is a non-myopic method that is based on the exploration/exploitation dilemma. Finally, we apply the principle of optimal active learning in MF and with some approximations, we derived a closed-form criterion. Moreover, we relax the assumption of full Oracle for new users and developed an active learning that exploits the characteristics of MF to choose items that are likely to be rated by new users.

- In chapter 7 we combine the power of matrix factorization with the easy-to-understand structure of decision trees to build adaptive questionnaires. It is called Factorized Decision Trees (FDT). First, decision trees are built. Then, a matrix factorization model is learned for rating prediction at leaf nodes. We propose a sampling method to speed up the tree construction algorithm. It is called Most Popular Sampling (MPS). Next, we upgrade 3-way split to 6-way split. It means, instead of considering three possible answers from new users, we consider six answers. This results in a more refined split and consequently, improves the accuracy. Finally, we improve FDT by initializing user and items features of MF in a way that exploits the structure of decision trees. It is called Warm FDT.

- In chapter 8 we introduce a new approach for active learning in recommender systems, which is called learning active learning. The main idea is to consider past users as (artificial) new users, in order to learn the right queries to be asked to new users for active-learning purposes. This constitutes a separate learning problem, in addition to the standard problem of predicting user ratings. We refer to this additional learning problem as 'learning active learning', since we develop a model that will be trained with ratings of past users in order to predict the right queries to be asked to (actual) new users. Based on this framework, we investigate two different types of models: the first model is based on information about average item ratings and the second on factorizing a matrix representing error reduction due to application of active learning.

- In chapter 9, we will discuss how active learning can be used for recommender systems in museums. In fact, this chapter shows how the theoretical achievements of this thesis can help us to overcome the difficulties that exist in real applications. We take our own project called RFID-Enhanced Museum for Interactive Experience (REMIX) (Karimi *et al.*, 2011d) as a museum recommender system. First, we describe REMIX and then we discuss how active learning can be leveraged to improve the quality of its recommendations.
- Finally we conclude the thesis and discuss possible directions of future research in chapter 10.

Chapter 2

Problem Definition

2.1 Active Learning for Recommender Systems

The most basic problem setting for active learning for recommender systems is as follows: given a set U called users, a set I called items and a set $R \subseteq \mathbb{R}$ called rating values, e.g., $R := \{1, 2, 3, 4, 5\}$, a number N called maximal number of queries to ask, furthermore given

- a set $\mathcal{D}^{\text{train}} \subseteq U \times I \times R$ of rating transactions as the training data,
- a target user $u \in U$ with the pool data $\mathcal{D}_u^{\text{pool}} \subseteq I \times R$ which contains at least N items he is able to rate, i.e $|D_u^{\text{pool}}| \geq N$,
- a recommendation model learning algorithm $\hat{r} : \mathcal{P}(U \times I \times R) \to \mathbb{R}^{U \times I}$ that learns for a given dataset $\mathcal{D} \subseteq U \times I \times R$ a recommendation model $\hat{r}_{\mathcal{D}} := \hat{r}(\mathcal{D})$ that can predict for every user u and item i a rating $\hat{r}_{\mathcal{D}}(u, i)$,
- an empirical risk function risk : $\mathcal{P}(U \times I \times R) \times \mathbb{R}^{U \times I} \to \mathbb{R}$ where $\text{risk}(\mathcal{D}, \hat{r})$ measures how badly model $\hat{r}$ predicts the ratings in dataset $\mathcal{D}$, e.g., $\text{risk}(\mathcal{D}, \hat{r}) := \frac{1}{|\mathcal{D}|} \sum_{(u,i,r) \in \mathcal{D}} \ell(r, \hat{r}(u, i))$ with a loss function $\ell : R \times \mathbb{R} \to \mathbb{R}$ where $\ell(r, \hat{r})$ measures how bad it is to predict a rating $\hat{r}$ if the true rating is r, e.g., $\ell(r, \hat{r}) := (r - \hat{r})^2$,

find sequentially items $i_1, \ldots, i_N \in \mathcal{D}_u^{\text{pool}}$ having access after each item i_j to its true rating $r(u, i_j)$ by the target user u, finally combined to a set $\mathcal{D}_u^{\text{query}} := \{(i_1, r(u, i_1)), \ldots, (i_N, r(u, i_N))\}$ of rating transactions, s.t. for a set $\mathcal{D}_u^{\text{test}} \subseteq I \times R$ of rating transactions (not accessible during training, drawn from the same underlying distribution), the empirical risk $\text{risk}(\mathcal{D}_u^{\text{test}}, \hat{r}_{\mathcal{D}^{\text{train}} \cup \mathcal{D}_u^{\text{query}}})$ of the recommendation model trained on the original rating transactions and the freshly queried rating transactions for the target user is minimal.

In this thesis, we solve the active learning problem for new users, i.e., when the target user u does not appear in the priori training data $\mathcal{D}^{\text{train}}$. Most approaches solve the problem by (i) computing in each step a score function $\hat{v} : \mathcal{D}_u^{\text{pool}} \to \mathbb{R}$ that predicts the information value of an item to be selected, and then (ii) selecting the one with highest predicted information value via a greedy strategy. Note that the above definition implies that the target user u is always able to rate the queried items, since $\mathcal{D}_u^{\text{pool}} \subseteq I \times R$ and R does not include missing value.

In this work, the profile of user u in $\mathcal{D}$ is denoted by

$$\mathcal{D}_u := \{(i, r) \in I \times R \mid (u, i, r) \in \mathcal{D}\}$$

Similarly the profile of item i in $\mathcal{D}$ is denoted by

$$\mathcal{D}_i := \{(u, r) \in U \times R \mid (u, i, r) \in \mathcal{D}\}$$

We denote that if the index of $\mathcal{D}$ is a user id, the result of $\mathcal{D}_u$ would be the corresponding user profile and if it is an item id, $\mathcal{D}_i$ refers to the corresponding item profile.

2.2 Datasets

In this work, three datasets are used: Movielens (100K), MovieRating, and Netflix. All datasets are for movie recommendation scenario. In order to have a fare comparison, in each experiment, we use the same dataset which has been used in the baseline. The first works on active learning for recommender systems conducted their experiments on the MovieLens and MovieRating datasets (Harpale & Yang, 2008; Jin & Si, 2004; Rashid *et al.*, 2002). As the Netflix became more popular, active learning works also switched on this dataset (Golbandi *et al.*, 2011; Zhou *et al.*, 2011). In each chapter, the same dataset as the baseline will be used.

In this section, the characteristics of these three datasets and the way they have been split are described.

2.2.1 MovieLens

MovieLens(100k)[1] dataset was collected by the GroupLens Research Project at the University of Minnesota[2]. This data set consists of:

- 100,000 ratings (1-5) from 943 users on 1682 movies
- Each user has rated at least 20 movies
- Simple demographic info for the users (age, gender, occupation, zip)

[1] http://www.grouplens.org/datasets/movielens/
[2] http://www.grouplens.org

The dataset was collected through the MovieLens web site[1] from September 19th, 1997 through April 22nd, 1998. This data has been cleaned up,i.e users who had less than 20 ratings or did not have complete demographic information were removed from this data set.

The dataset is randomly split into training and test sets. The training dataset consists of 343 users (the same number used in (Jin & Si, 2004)) and the rest of users are in the test dataset. Each test user is considered as a new user. The latent features of the new user are initially trained with three random ratings (again the same number used in the (Jin & Si, 2004)). 20 rated items of each test user are separated to compute the error. The test items are not new item and already appeared in the training data. The remaining items are in the pool dataset, i.e the dataset that is used to select a query. In our experiment, 10 queries are asked from each new user. Therefore, the pool dataset should contain at east 10 items which exist in the training data. Considering 10 queries, 3 initial random seeds, and 20 test items, each test user has given ratings to at least 33 items. In the case there are test users with less amount of ratings, the split is simply ignored and a new one is found. In our experiments, usually after three trials the training and test splits containing all dataset users are found. As this data sets is rather small, the experiments are done based in 10-fold cross validation.

2.2.2 MovieRating

MovieRating[2] includes movie ratings collected through user interactions with the MovieLens site [3]. The difference between this dataset and the MovieLens is not clear. It seems that MovieLens has been built based on MovieRating. Although MovieRating can be still downloaded from the website, but it is no longer used in the recent papers. This dataset includes ratings on the scale of 1 (worst) to 5 (best) by 500 users of 1000 movies.

The dataset is randomly split into training and test sets. The training dataset consists of 200 users (the same number used in the baseline (Jin & Si, 2004)) and 300 users are in the test dataset. The rest of details on splitting are the same as MovieLens dataset.

2.2.3 Netflix

This dataset was used for Netflix prize[4]. It includes movie ratings of 480,189 users gave to 17,770 movies. The number of ratings is 100,480,507 where each training rating is a quadruplet of the form <user, movie, date of rating, rating>. The dataset is already split as follows:

- Training set (99,072,112 ratings not including the probe set, 100,480,507 including the probe set)

[1] http://movielens.umn.edu

[2] http://rp-www.cs.usyd.edu.au/ irena/movie_data.zip

[3] http:// www.movielens.org

[4] http://www.netflixprize.com/

- Probe set (1,408,395 ratings) for hyper-parameter search
- Qualify set (2,817,131 ratings) consisting of:
  - Test set (1,408,789 ratings), used to determine winners
  - Quiz set (1,408,342 ratings), used to calculate leaderboard scores

The probe, quiz, and test data sets have similar statistical characteristics. Also, the title and year of release of the movies are provided in a separate dataset. It should be mentioned that Netflix is not longer available to download.

The way that Netflix has been split is not suitable for cold-start evaluation protocol since users in the training and test sets are the same. As test users are considered to be new users, they should not already appear in the training set. Therefore, we split all users into two disjoint subsets, the training set and the test set, containing 75% and 25% users, respectively. The ratings of training users in the training set (including probe set) are used for training data. And the ratings of those users in the qualify set are used to find hyper-parameters. The ratings of test users in the qualify set are used to generate the user responses in the interview process (pool data). To evaluate the performance after each query, the ratings of test users in the qualify set are used.

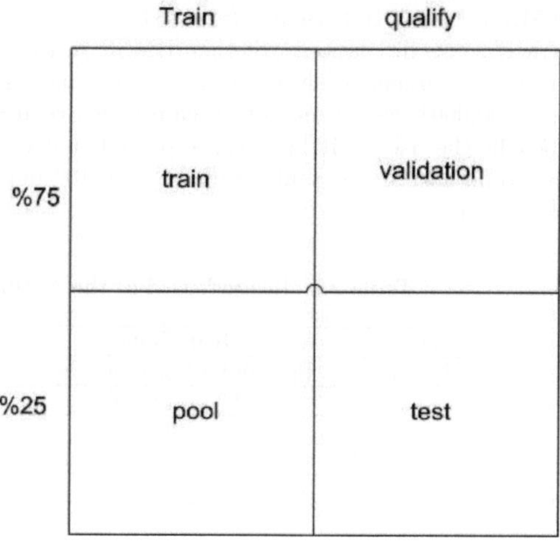

Figure 2.1: Netflix dataset is split into four sets: train, validation, pool, and test sets.

2.3 Evaluation Protocol

The main challenge in applying active learning for recommender systems is that users are not willing to answer many queries in order to rate the queried items. For this reason, we report the performance of all examined methods in terms of prediction error (RMSE or MAE) versus the number of queried items, which is simply denoted as the *number of queries*. The RMSE of user u is computed as follows:

$$RMSE_u = \sqrt{\frac{1}{|\mathcal{D}_u^{test}|} \sum_{(i,r) \in \mathcal{D}_u^{test}} (r - \hat{r}_{ui})^2} \tag{2.1}$$

where $\mathcal{D}_u^{test}$ is the set of the test items of user u, $\hat{r}_{ui}$ is the predicted rating of user u for item i, and r_{ui} is the true (actual) rating. Thus, we examine the problem of selecting at each step, the item for which each new user u will be queried to provide a rating. Also, Mean Absolute Error (MAE) is expressed as follows:

$$MAE_u = \frac{1}{|\mathcal{D}_u^{test}|} \sum_{(i,r) \in \mathcal{D}_u^{test}} |r - \hat{r}_{ui}| \tag{2.2}$$

The RMSE and MAE of each test user is measured separately and then the average RMSE or MAE over all test users is reported.

There was some discussions whether RMSE is the right metric to evaluate the performance of recommender systems. This question raised after the Netflix prize. In this prize, 1,000,000$ was given to the team which reduced the RMSE by 10%. Does it really benefit the users? It has been reported that even 1% lift in RMSE leads to a significant difference in the ranking of the "top-10" most recommended movies for a user (Koren, 2007).

Table 2.1: Leaderboard of the Netflix Prize

Rank	Team Name	Score
1	BellKor's Pragmatic Chaos	0.8567
2	The Ensemble	0.8567
3	Grand Prize Team	0.8582
4	Opera Solutions and Vandelay United	0.8588
5	Vandelay Industries !	0.8591

Table 2.1 shows the score of the top five leaders of the Netflix Prize[1]. Clearly, the competition among them is very tough because the amount of improvement is the third or fourth digit after point. In this thesis, nevertheless, we will also observe the

[1] http://www.netflixprize.com/leaderboard

same phenomenon in our experiments. It shows that if we choose a strong baseline, we cannot expect a huge lift in improving the accuracy.

Chapter 3

Background

In this chapter, we provide the background knowledge that are needed to understand this thesis. As this thesis is about the application of active learning for recommender systems, this chapter addresses different aspects of active learning and recommender systems.

3.1 Active Learning

Traditionally, machine learning techniques fall into two categories: supervised and unsupervised. Later, semi-supervised learning was introduced. It aims to train a model using both a small labeled dataset and a large set of unlabeled data (Chapelle *et al.*, 2006). Therefore, it falls between supervised and unsupervised machine learning. Active learning, compared to semi-supervised learning, is one step closer to supervised learning. In active learning, in addition to labeled and unlabeled data, there is a possibility to ask the labels of unlabeled data from the Oracle. Oracle is the one who knows the labels. Figure 3.1 shows the place of active learning among other kinds of machine learning techniques.

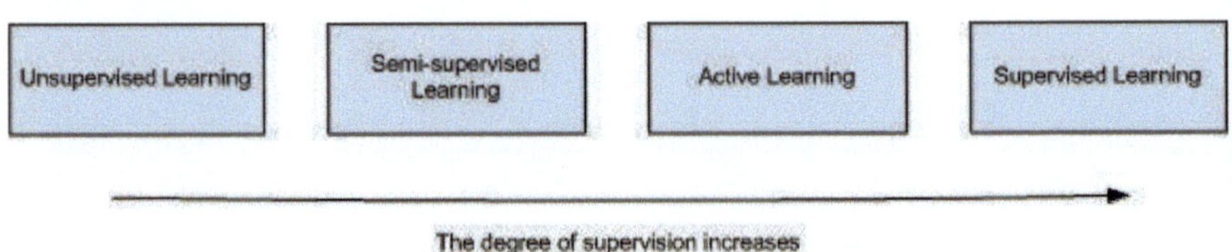

Figure 3.1: The place of active learning compared to other types of machine learning techniques.

In general, active learning consists of four steps: selecting a query, asking the query from the Oracle, adding the new instance to the training data, and updating the model. Figure 3.2 shows these steps.

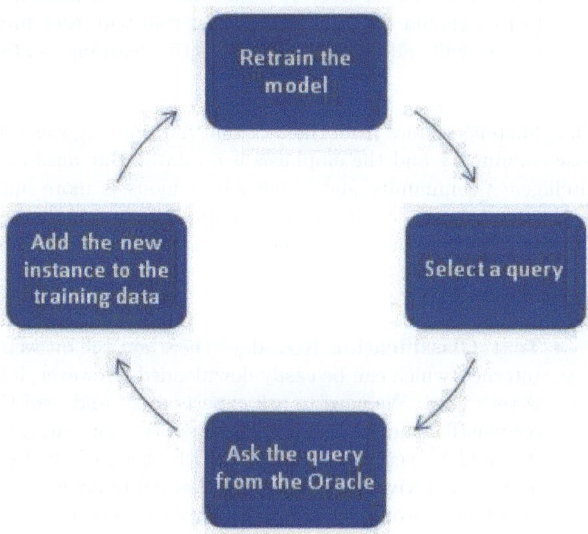

Figure 3.2: Four steps of active learning: selecting a query, asking the query from the Oracle, adding new instance to the training data, and updating the model

Active Learning (AL) can be studied from two angles: data mining and machine learning. Although the developed techniques are the same, but the motivations are different:

- **Active Learning in Data Mining:** there is a learner who wants to learn from experiences. The experiences have already been collected and stored in a dataset. The amount of labeled data in the dataset is small, so the learner cannot learn enough from the dataset. The learner has the option to ask the missing labels from an Oracle who knows the labels. But querying the labels is costly for the learner. Therefore, the learner selects a limited number of instances for query. The instances should be informative. It means they will improve the performance of the learner significantly, so it is worth it to pay the query cost for the learner. Later in this chapter, we will call this definition of active learning as *pool-based* active learning.

- **Active Learning in Machine Learning:** there is a learner who wants to learn from experiences. The experiences are not necessarily already exist. The learner is active (autonomous) and is able to collect the experiences on his own. Experiencing is not for free. It needs time, effort, money, and so on. Therefore, the learner should try those experiences that will teach him a lot. Later in this chapter, we will call this definition of active learning as *stream-based* active learning.

This difference comes from the fact that data mining was originally developed by data base community and the emphasis is on data. But machine learning is from artificial intelligence community and being autonomous is more important. Despite different motivations, both definitions are identical if we treat experience as unlabeled data. Therefore, in this thesis we do not distinguish between them.

3.1.1 Examples

- **Text Classification** Nowadays there are billion web pages and documents on Internet, which can be easily downloaded. However, labeling that amount of data is very hard. We need to ask experts to sit and read the whole of a document to see whether the document is about sport, economy, science, and so on. Therefore, it would be very useful to reduce the need of labeled data without loosing the accuracy. Active learning selects a subset of documents that providing their label by a human would substantially improve the accuracy of the model. It saves a lot of experts' time while the accuracy of the model is almost the same as a model that has been trained with the full dataset (Godbole *et al.*, 2004; Tong & Koller, 2002; Yang *et al.*, 2009).

- **Visual Object Detection:** Machine learning methods have been vastly used for visual object detection (Destrero *et al.*, 2007; Li & Zhang, 2004; Viola & Jones, 2001; Zhang & Zhang, 2010). Usually, these methods need a large set of training data to work. An important observation is that while the prediction models are able to provide accurate predictions for objects that are obvious, they fail to detect objects that are similar (Abramson & Freund, 2005). Those objects are objects that pose higher uncertainty for the model. Therefore, instead of spending a lot of effort to collect a large set of labeled data, it is reasonable to annotate only a limited set of data that models are uncertain about their labels.

- **Speech Recognition:** Obtaining unlabeled speech data is easy. You just need to put a microphone somewhere and record the voice. However, labeling this data is difficult. Somebody needs to look at the voice's wave and annotate it. Furthermore, not all voice instances are really useful for labeling. If a speech instance is clear enough, it can be predicted well by the prediction model and there is no need for annotating it. But instances that are similar or noisy are informative and are good candidates for annotation (Riccardi & Hakkani-Tr, 2003, 2005; Yu *et al.*, 2010).

- **Robotics:** Robots are usually equipped with Reinforcement Learning (RL) (Sutton & Barto, 1998b) to learn how to act in an unknown environment. RL is based on exploration/exploitation dilemma. First robots discover the environment by exploration and then exploit the learned knowledge. Active learning can speed up the exploration phase by selecting actions that are more informative. It means robots learn a lot after doing such action (Akiyama *et al.*, 2010; Epshteyn *et al.*, 2008; Lopes *et al.*, 2009).

- **Computational Drug Design:** the goal of computational drug design is to find compounds that can bind to a target molecule. In each iteration a batch of unlabeled compounds is tested against the molecule. The goal in each iteration is to find as many as possible compounds that match the target molecule. Those compounds are called "active" and others are called" passive". To know the label (active or passive) of each compound, chemists need to do some experiments, which needs effort, time, and money. It means collecting the data is costly. As the result, the problem fits well with the characteristics of active learning (Warmuth *et al.*, 2001).

3.1.2 Scenarios

Active learning algorithms are studied in three major scenarios (Settles, 2010):

- **Pool-based active learning**: there is a pool of independent and identically distributed unlabeled instances. At each iteration, the learner selects one or more instances and ask their labels from the Oracle. After receiving the labels, the learner updated the prediction model and selects new instances for query. This is also called as *selective sampling* (Lewis & Gale, 1994). Most of active learning methods are pool-based. For example, text classification (Hoi *et al.*, 2006a; Lewis & Gale, 1994; Nicholas & McCallum, 2001; Tong & Koller, 2000a), information extraction (Settles & Craven, 2008; Thompson *et al.*, 1999), image classification and retrieval (Tong & Chang, 2001; Zhang & Chen, 2002), video classification (Hauptmann *et al.*, 2006; Yan *et al.*, 2003), speech recognition (Tur *et al.*, 2005), and cancer diagnosis (Liu, 2004).

- **Stream-based active learning:** Given sampling data is for free, the learner first samples an instance from the actual distribution and then decides whether to query its label (Cohn *et al.*, 1994). Sometimes instead of only one instance, a stream of instances are sampled. In this case, each sample is still evaluated for querying independent of other instances (Angluin, 1988). A naive way of selecting an instance for query is to set a minimum threshold on an informativeness measure and instances whose evaluation is above this threshold are queried. A more advanced method is to make a biased random decision such that more informative instances are more likely to be queried (Argamon-Engelson & Dagan, 1999). The stream-based scenario has been studied in several real-world applications, including speech recognition (Argamon-Engelson & Dagan, 1999), sensor scheduling (Krishnamurthy, 2002), learning ranking functions for information retrieval (Yu, 2005), and word sense disambiguation (Fujii *et al.*, 1998). Selective Sampling is another name of stream-based active learning (Atlas *et al.*, 1990).

- **Active learning with membership queries:** It is the first proposed scenario for active learning (Angluin, 1988). In this setting, the leaner generates the instances on his own by imposing values on attributes rather than sampling from an underlying distribution. (Cohn *et al.*, 1995) developed active learning methods for two statistical models: mixture of Gaussian and locally weighted. They conducted the experiments on robots manipulators. Other related works include handwriting recognition (Lang & Baum, 1992), finite concept class (Angluin, 2001), and biology (King *et al.*, 2004). The drawback of active learning with membership queries is that the the generated queries might not be meaningful. For example, (Lang & Baum, 1992) applies membership queries to train a neural network to classify handwritten characters. They report that many of the query images generated by the learner are not recognizable by humans. They are only artificial hybrid characters that had no natural semantic meaning.

All three types of active learning scenarios suppose that collecting unlabeled data is for free. However, some authors extend active learning for situations where, in addition to labeling data, collecting data is also costly. (Krause & Guestrin, 2007; Leskovec *et al.*, 2007) study where to install sensors to collect data about rivers or water distribution networks. As installing sensors is costly, one needs to choose specific places where collecting data is crucial to observe the behavior of the phenomena. This scenario is not consistent with any of the active learning scenarios: there is not a pool of unlabeled data, sampling an instance from the distribution is not for free, and generating data by the learner is not also for free. Therefore, it not clear whether such problems are really active learning problems.

3.1.3 Criteria

The aim of active learning is to choose a query that would reduce the test error of the model as much as possible. To reach this goal, a bunch of criteria (sometimes is called heuristic, strategy, or policy) have been proposed (Settles, 2010). In this section, we briefly review the most important ones.

Uncertainty

The simplest and most commonly used strategy to choose a query is uncertainty sampling. Specifically, the learner queries the instances that it is least certain about their labels. The definition of uncertainty depends on the learner's prediction model. In the case of the Naive Base model applied to binary classification, where for each test instance the model produces a probability in the range $[0, 1]$, uncertainty is low when the probability is closer to 0 or 1 (i.e., when the classifier can decide more certainly), whereas uncertainty is high when the probability is closer to 0.5 (i.e., when the classifier cannot certainly decide) (Lewis & Catlett, 1994; Lewis & Gale, 1994). For more complex data structures, one needs to define the uncertainty based on Entropy (Shannon, 1948). For example, (Settles & Craven, 2008) developed active learning for sequence and (Hwa, 2004) defined uncertainty for decision trees. An alternative to entropy for these complex structures is *least confident* (Culotta & McCallum, 2005; Lafferty *et al.*, 2001).

Uncertainty criterion may also be used with non-probabilistic models. In SVM classifier (Cortes & Vapnik, 1995), instances that are close to decision boundary pose higher uncertainty (Tong & Koller, 2000b). In the case of using ensemble learning, the uncertainty is the amount of disagreement on the label of instances. It is also called Query-by-Committee (Abe & Mamitsuka, 1998; Melville & Mooney, 2004; Seung *et al.*, 1992). For kNN, each neighbor votes on the class label of instance x. The proportion of these votes represent the posterior label probability (Fujii *et al.*, 1998; Lindenbaum *et al.*, 2004), which is then used to define uncertainty. (Lewis & Catlett, 1994) develops decision trees that in addition to predicting labels, are also able to provide the posterior probabilities. The probabilities are then used to define uncertainty of examples.

Optimal

In active learning, the optimal query is one that reduces the test error as much as possible. However, finding such a query is not possible because of two reasons. First, the distribution of the test data is unknown. Second, the labels are not known before querying. However, there are some works that stick with the principal of optimal active learning and try to overcome the difficulties by relying on some assumptions and then develop methods for specific models that approximate the optimal active learning. (Cohn *et al.*, 1995) proposed one of the first statistical analyses of active learning. They came up with a solution that minimizes the test error by minimizing the learner variance. We will explain this method in chapter 4.

Later, (Zhang & Oles, 2000) proposed a similar approach for selecting optimal queries in a pool-based setting for classifiers based on Fisher information (Schervish, 1995). (Hoi *et al.*, 2006a) extended this approach to active learning for text classification in the batch-mode setting in which all queries are selected at once.

Expected Error Reduction

Direct Approximation of the optimal active learning does not always lead to a closed-form solution. An alternative is to estimate the expected future error that would result if some new instance is labeled and added to the training data. And the best instance is the one that minimizes that expectation. (Nicholas & McCallum, 2001) was the first paper in this direction. They used Naive Bays classifier and applied it for text classification. This approach has also been applied to SVM (Moskovitch *et al.*, 2007), logistic regression (Guo & Greiner, 2007), and semi-supervised learning (Zhu *et al.*, 2003).

Expected Model Change

Traditional learning methods like simulated annealing (Kirkpatrick *et al.*, 1983) start the learning process by exploring the solution (parameter) space. The reason of that is to avoid local optimal. The same principal is also valid for statistical machine learning methods that have been trained with a small training dataset. Adding an instance to the training data that would impart the greatest change to the current model, leads to exploring the parameters space and avoids local minimum. For discriminative probabilistic models that use Stochastic Gradient Descent (SGD) (Vapnik & Chervonenkis, 1971), the expected change in the model is equal to the expected change in the gradient (Settles & Craven, 2008; Settles *et al.*, 2008).

Density

In machine learning it is assumed that the distribution of the training data and test data are the same. This assumption is more likely holds when there are enough training data to cover the whole of the data space. But in the case of active learning this assumption may be invalid since there are already few labeled data. This problem affects the accuracy of the prediction model. Some active learning methods aim to improve the accuracy of the model by choosing instances that are heterogeneous in the sense that they are from different parts of the data space. Adding such instances to the training data would likely make the distribution of the training data closer to the distribution of the test data. Density-weighted active learning methods first cluster instances and then choose instances that not only are uncertain, but also are "representative" of the input distribution. In this way, we ensue that an instance from all clusters are selected. Also, instances that belong to dense clusters would have higher chances to be selected (Dasgupta & Hsu, 2008; Nguyen & Smeulders, 2004; Settles & Craven, 2008; Xu *et al.*, 2007).

3.1.4 Settings

Serial vs. Batch Active Learning

Usually active learning methods select one query at a time. However, if training the prediction model is expensive, it is more efficient to query a batch of instances and then retrain the model with all of them. The benefit of this approach is that it is faster and also it requires fewer interactions with the Oracle. But still it has its own difficulties. Selecting the "N-best" queries according to a given query selection criterion often does not work well, since it fails to consider the overlap in information content among the "best" instances. To overcome this problem (Brinker, 2003) developed a batch-mode active learning for SVM in which diversity among instances in a batch is considered. (Xu *et al.*, 2007), instead of diversity, incorporate density in the batch. (Hoi *et al.*, 2006a,b) extended the Fisher information framework (Schervish, 1995) to the batch-mode setting for binary logistic regression. (Guo & Schuurmans, 2007) considered the batch construction as an optimization problem and solved it for the binary logistic regression. Notably, in the experiments of these papers random sampling works better than "N-best" sampling.

Myopic vs. Non-myopic Active Learning

Usually active learning methods are greedy (myopic). They suppose that the next query is the last query and try to find the best one. However, a greedy solution is not an optimal solution for active learning problems. The optimal solution is one that finds the best *sequence* of queries. To the best of our knowledge, there is no paper that *explicitly* treats active learning as a non-myopic problem. (Poupart, March 2009) proposed a general idea on applying Reinforcement Learning (RL) for active learning problem. The idea explicitly models the sequence of queries with a Markov Decision Process (MDP) and learns the best sequence of queries with RL. The speaker did not do any experiment in this regard and suggested to apply it for realistic assistive technology (Ibbme *et al.*, 2005). In order to apply this idea to the pool-based active learning problem, one should define state, action, and a reward function according to the characteristics of active learning, which is non-trivial.

There are some papers that are implicitly non-myopic. Implicitly means that they do not find the best sequence of queries but still suppose that the next query is not the last query. Therefore, sometimes they explore the data space in the hope of discovering an instance that at end, querying its label would be beneficial, though it is not the best instance for the next query. (Baram *et al.*, 2004) proposed Kernel Farthest First (KFF), which chooses instances that are far from decision boundary. All methods that incorporate density into query selection criterion are also somewhat non-myopic (Dasgupta & Hsu, 2008; Nguyen & Smeulders, 2004; Settles & Craven, 2008; Xu *et al.*, 2007).

Although RL has not significantly contributed in the literature of AL, but there are a couple of papers that acted in the other way around. Specifically, they use active learning to reduce the amount of exploration in RL. It means instead of relying on arbitrary states, only those states and actions that are expected to be part of the optimal decision are experienced (Epshteyn *et al.*, 2008; Lopes *et al.*, 2009; Teytaud *et al.*, 2007) .

3.1.5 Algorithm

Consider the problem of learning a binary classifier on a partially labeled database $\mathcal{D} \subseteq X \times Y$ in which $\{x_1, ..., x_n\} \subset \mathbb{R}^d$ are instances and $y \in \{-1, +1\}$ are labels.

The training data $\mathcal{D}^{\text{train}}$ is divided into labeled $\mathcal{D}^{label}$ and pool data $\mathcal{D}^{pool}$. First, the classifier $\hat{f}: X \to Y$ is trained with $\mathcal{D}^{label}$ using the learning algorithm F:

$$\begin{aligned} F: f(X \times Y) \longmapsto & \quad Y^X \\ D \longmapsto & \quad (\hat{f}: X \to Y) \end{aligned}$$

Then active learning selects N instances x from pool data $\mathcal{D}^{pool}$ and asks their label $f(x)$ from an oracle. The goal of active learning is to select queries that will result in maximum gained accuracy after retraining the classifier with the queried instances.

In myopic active learning, it is supposed that the next query is the last query, so the instance that is *likely* to be the best one is selected. The selection is done based on an objective function (we call it selection function σ in this paper):

$$\begin{aligned} \sigma: X \times Y^X & \longmapsto R \\ (x, \hat{f}) & \longmapsto \sigma(x, \hat{f}) \end{aligned}$$

σ depends on the current classifier $\hat{f}$. The best query is one that minimizes σ:

$$x^* = \underset{x \in D^{pool}}{\operatorname{argmin}} \, \sigma(x, \hat{f})$$

Usually one query is selected in each iteration. This process repeats until N queries are selected. The general algorithm of active learning is presented in Algorithm 1. First, the model is trained with the available labeled data. In a special case of active learning there is no labeled data at all. It is called vanilla AL. In this case, the model parameters are initialized randomly.

Algorithm 1 The general algorithm of active learning

Input: N, $\mathcal{D}^{label}$, $\mathcal{D}^{pool}$, F
Output: $\hat{f}, \mathcal{D}^{query}$
  Train $\hat{f}$ on $\mathcal{D}^{label}$: $\hat{f} := F(\mathcal{D}^{label})$
  $\mathcal{D}^{query} := \emptyset$
  for $i \in 1, .., N$ **do**
    $x^* := \text{argmax}_{x \in \mathcal{D}^{pool}} \, \sigma(x, \hat{f})$
    remove x^* from D^{pool}
    $\mathcal{D}^{query} := \mathcal{D}^{query} \dot{\cup} \{x^*\}$
    Query y from Oracle : $y := f(x^*)$ *(label of* x^**)*
    $\mathcal{D}^{query} := \mathcal{D}^{query} \dot{\cup} \{(x^*, y)\}$
    $\hat{f} := F(\mathcal{D}^{label} \dot{\cup} \mathcal{D}^{query})$
  end for

3.2 Recommendation Algorithms

After introducing recommender systems in the introduction chapter, we explain the details of several recommendation techniques that later will be used in this thesis. Then, we will discuss the challenges of cold-start recommendation.

3.2.1 Simple Baselines

There are a couple of methods that are too simple to be used in practice, but they are good for comparison purposes. If one comes up with a new idea that is worse than these methods, either the idea is wrong or there is a bug in the implementation. Another benefit of these baselines is that they are fast. If there is a complicated method that is slow and does not gain too much accuracy compare to these baselines, the method is not worth it to be used. The trivial methods for rating prediction and item recommendation are as follows:

Rating Prediction

- **Global Average:** it is simply the average over all observed ratings of the dataset. In this way, a same value is predicted for all missing ratings.
- **User (Item) average:** A user (an item) receives the same prediction for all missing ratings. The prediction is the average over all observed ratings of the user (item).

Item Recommendation

- **Random:** A set of items are randomly selected for recommendation.
- **Most Popular:** Items that have received most ratings from users are recommended. Another definition of most popular items is that items that have been *liked* by many users. In the movie recommendation scenario, like means ratings 4 or 5 out of 5. In this thesis, we stick with the first definition.

3.2.2 Nearest-Neighbor

Nearest-Neighbor (NN) method in Collaborative Filtering (CF) is similar to Nearest-Neighbor technique in machine learning. In user-based NN, to predict the rating of user u to item i, a subset of users who have rated item i and are similar to users u are selected. The prediction is the weighted average over all ratings of similar users to item i in which the weights are normalized similarities. Symmetrically, in item-based NN, a subset of items that have been rated by user u and are similar to item i are selected. The prediction is the weighted average over all ratings of similar items by user u in which the weights are normalized similarities.

The similarity between users is measured through Pearson correlation (Breese *et al.*, 1998):

$$w(u,v) = \frac{\sum_i (r_{ui} - \bar{R_u})(r_{vi} - \bar{R_v})}{\sqrt{\sum_i (r_{ui} - \bar{R_u})^2 \sum_i (r_{vi} - \bar{R_v})^2}} \tag{3.1}$$

where w_{uv} is the similarity between user u and user v, $\bar{R_u}$ and $\bar{R_v}$ are the average of ratings of users u and v respectively, and the summations over i are over the items that both users u and v have rated. Symmetrically, the similarities between items can be measured.

After computing the similarities, we can predict the missing ratings. The predictions are the weighted sum over all observed ratings in which the weights are the similarities:

$$\hat{r}_{ui} = \frac{\sum_v w_{uv} r_{vi}}{\sum_v |w_{uv}|} \tag{3.2}$$

3.2.3 Aspect Model

Aspect Model (AM) is one of the first successful model-based techniques for CF (Hofmann, 2003; Hofmann & Puzicha, 1999). It measures the probability of observing the tuple (u,i,r) as follows:

$$p(r|i,u) = \sum_{f \in Z} p(r|f,i) P(f|u) \tag{3.3}$$

where $P(f|u)$ is the likelihood that user u is in class f and $p(r|f,i)$ is the likelihood of receiving rating r for item i by users in class f, and Z is the set of all possible classes. Given the latent factors $\{f_1, f_2, ..., f_k\}$, the AM supposes that users and items are independent from each other. If $p(r|f,i)$ is assumed to be a Gaussian model, we would have Gaussian mixture model with user-specific mixing weights :

$$p(r|i,u) = \sum_{f \in Z} P(f|u) p(r; \mu_{i,f}, \sigma_{i,f}) \tag{3.4}$$

where

$$p(r; \mu, \sigma) = \frac{1}{\sqrt{2\pi}\sigma} \exp[-\frac{(r-\mu)^2}{2\sigma^2}] \tag{3.5}$$

$\mu_{i,f}$ and $\sigma_{i,f}$ of $p(r;\mu,\sigma)$ are computed as follows:

$$\mu_{i,f} = \frac{\sum_{\langle u,i',r\rangle : i'=i} rP(f|u,r,i)}{\sum_{\langle u,i',r\rangle : i'=i} P(f|u,r,i)} \tag{3.6}$$

$$\sigma^2_{i,f} = \frac{\sum_{\langle u,i',r\rangle : i'=i} (r-\mu_{i,f})^2 P(f|u,r,i)}{\sum_{\langle u,i',r\rangle : i'=i} P(f|u,r,i)} \tag{3.7}$$

Usually the ratings of each user are normalized to be a normal distribution with zero mean and variance as 1. Also, the model parameters θ are learned using Expectation Maximization (Hastie *et al.*, 2001) learning algorithm. As in this thesis, we deal with the new user problem, we define the parameters space based on the user parameters as follows:

$$\theta_u = \{\theta_{u_f} : \theta_{u_f} = P(f|u), \forall f \in Z\}$$

3.2.4 Matrix Factorization

Matrix Factorization (MF) is the task of approximating the true, unobserved ratings-matrix R by $\hat{R} : \mathbb{R}^{|U|\times|I|}$ where U is the set of users and I is the set of items. It maps both users and items to a latent space of dimensionality k. In this space, user-item interactions are modeled as inner products. In the latent space, each item i is represented with a vector $h_i \in \mathbb{R}^k$. The elements of h_i indicate the importance of factors in rating item i by users. Some factors might have higher effect and vice versa. In the same way, each user u is represented with a vector $w_u \in \mathbb{R}^k$ in the latent space. For a given user the element of w_u measure the influence of the factors on user preferences. Different applications of MF differ in the constraints that are sometimes imposed on the factorization. The most common form of MF is finding a low-rank approximation (unconstrained factorization) to a fully observed data matrix minimizing the sum-squared difference to it.

The resulting dot product, $h_i^T w_u$, captures the interaction between user u and item i. However, the full rating value is not just explained by this interaction and the user and item bias should also be taken into account. This is because part of the rating values is due to effects associated with either users or items, i.e biases, independent of any interactions. By considering the user and item bias, the predicted rating is computed as follows (Koren *et al.*, 2009):

$$\hat{r}_{ui} = \mu + b_i + b_u + h_i^T w_u \tag{3.8}$$

where μ is the global average, b_i is the item bias and b_u is the user bias.

Figure 3.3 shows a simple example of MF for movie recommendation scenario. There are two latent dimensions. The first dimension measures female- versus male-oriented characteristic and the second dimension deals with serious versus escapist aspect. In general, the predicted ratings of users for items is proportional to their distances in this space. For example, we expect that Guss gives a high rating to "Dumb and Dumber" and a low rating to "The Color Purple". Or if study this figure from recommendation point of view, "Dumb and Dumber" is a good recommendation for Guss and "The Color Purple" is a bad recommendation.

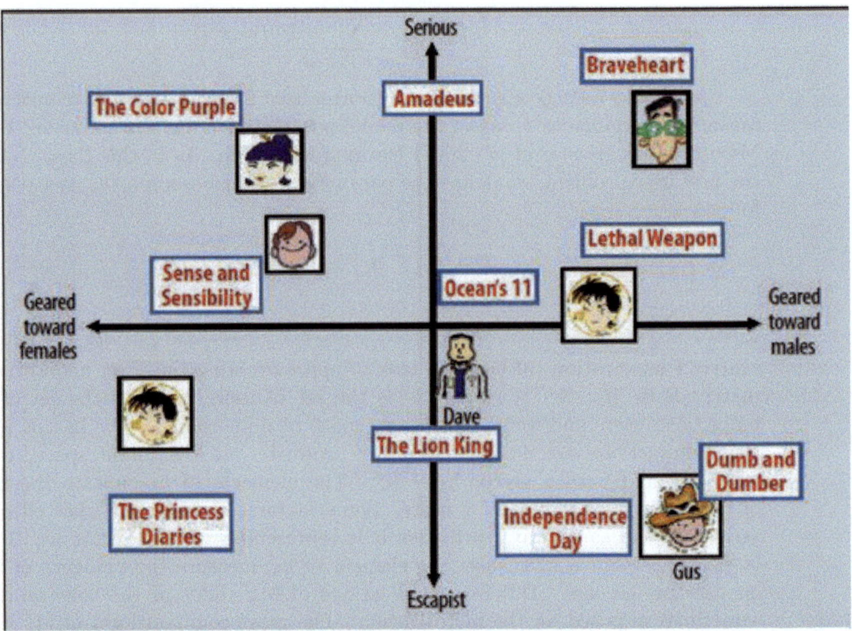

Figure 3.3: A simple two dimensional latent space for movie recommendation scenario. The figure is from (Koren *et al.*, 2009)

The major challenge is computing the mapping of each item and user to factor vectors $h_i, w_u \in \mathbb{R}^k$. The mapping is done by minimizing the following squared error (Koren, 2008):

$$Opt(\mathcal{D}^{\text{train}}, W, H) = \sum_{(u,i,r)\in\mathcal{D}^{\text{train}}} \left((r_{ui} - \mu - b_u - b_i - h_i^T w_u)^2 + \lambda(\|h_i\|^2 + |w_u\|^2) + \gamma(b_i^2 + b_u^2) \right) \tag{3.9}$$

where λ is the regularization factor, and $\mathcal{D}^{\text{train}}$ is the set of the (u, i, r) pairs for which r_{ui} is known, i.e the training set $\mathcal{D}^{\text{train}}$. The usual method to train MF is stochastic gradient descent (Koren *et al.*, 2009). This algorithm shuffles the ratings and then loops through all of them by picking a random triple (u, i, r) and updates the corresponding parameters in equation 3.9. After each epoch, the error of the loss function is computed and then compared to the error of the previous epoch. If the difference of the errors is smaller than ϵ, the training stops. Otherwise it continues until at most L iterations.

When MF is applied to a specific data set, the predicted ratings should be in the range of the minimum rating and maximum rating of the dataset. However, sometimes this does not happen and we have to explicitly clip them. To solve this problem we use the sigmoidal function to automatically truncate the predicted rating to the range of minimum and maximum ratings. Therefore, the predicted ratings are computed as follows:

$$\hat{r}_{ui} = MinRating + \frac{(MaxRating - MinRating)}{1 + e^{-(\mu + b_i + b_u + h_i^T w_u)}} \tag{3.10}$$

Note that the sigmoidal function is plugged-in to the optimization function 3.9 as well, which results in a new derivation.

When a new user enters the recommender system, the predictive model should be updated to learn the new user latent features. As there are already a lot of users in the recommender system, training the model from scratch needs a lot of time. Therefore, we switch to online updating and develop the active learning algorithm based on that. Online updating means after a first training with all users, further retraining is only done for new users. For online updating, we use the method introduced in (Rendle & Schmidt-Thieme, 2008). In this method after getting a new rating for a new user, the user's latent features are initialized to a random setting and then learned using all ratings of the new user. The details of this method is described in Algorithm 2.

Algorithm 2 Online updating for new-user problem (Rendle & Schmidt-Thieme, 2008)

initialize $u^\star$-th row in W
repeat
loop {repeats until the stopping criteria is met}
    for $r_{ui} \in \mathcal{D}_u^{\text{train}}$ **do**
        for $f \leftarrow 1, ..., k$ **do**
            $w_{uf} \leftarrow w_{uf} - \alpha \frac{\partial}{\partial w_{uf}} Opt(\mathcal{D}, W, H)$
        end for
    end for
end loop
return (W,H)

3.2.5 Cold-Start Recommendation

CF suffers from a sever problem that is called cold-start problem. To understand this problem, first we provide an example on how CF works in general and then extend this example for cold-start problem.

	Mummy	Matrix	Avator	Iron Man	Titanic	Terminator
Andy	4	5		5		2
Bill	2	1		3		5
Katrin		5				2
Judy						

Figure 3.4: An example for Cold-start recommendation

Figure 3.4 shows a simple example of CF for movie recommendation scenario. Suppose that we want to predict the rating of Katrin for Iron Man. If we compare the profile of Katrin with Andy, we will notice that they have a very similar taste. Both like Matrix and dislike Terminator. Therefore, it is expected that Katrin like Andy would like Iron Man. In contrast, if Katrin and Bill have different opinions about Matrix and Terminator. Therefore, it is not reasonable to use the ratings of Bill to predict the missing ratings of Katrin. Now Judy enters the system. As she has not given any ratings, system cannot predict ratings, and consequently recommend items, for her in a personalized fashion. This problem is called *new user problem.* There are different approaches to deal with this problem. We can simply skip CF and switch to other methods until Judy rates a couple of ratings. For example, most popular item recommendation, random recommendation, or recommendation based on implicit feedback (Zhang *et al.*, 2009; Zigoris, 2006).

Another solution for this problem is to ask Judy to rate a few movies so that the system learns a little about her preferences. By passing the time and getting more ratings from Judy, the system also improves its initial knowledge about Judy's preferences. Now the question is that which movies are good candidates to be queried by Judy. Suppose that we ask her to rate Avator or Titanic. These queries are useless because other three users have not rated them. Therefore, we cannot find similar users to Judy based on her rating to these movies. But Mummy is a good query because it has been rated by Andy and Bill.

The aim of active learning for new user problem in recommender systems is to identify items that when they are queried by new users, their ratings will help to learn new users preferences as much as possible. In this thesis, we will investigate different approaches to achieve this goal. We will start with the settings in which new users are able to rate all queried items. Next, we relax this assumption and suppose that new users are allowed not to rate items that they do not know them.

Chapter 4

Related Work

In this chapter we first summarize the related work on active learning for supervised machine learning. Most of the related works on active learning have already been introduced in chapter 3. In this chapter we only focus on the works that have influenced active learning for recommender systems and explain them in more details. Next, we focus on the related work that applies active learning in recommender systems.

4.1 Active Learning for Supervised Machine Learning

Most of the related work on active learning for supervised machine learning fall in the category of classification. The reason is that the Oracle, who provides the labels, is usually a human. And for humans it is easier to work on names than numbers. For example, if you ask somebody what the exact temperature is, she may not know that. But she can say whether she feels cold or hot. Moreover, the applications that demand active learning technique are mostly classification problems. For example, document classification. There is a large set of unlabeled documents. In the other hand, labeling documents is not for free because we have to pay money to some experts to read them and tell us what they are about.

4.1.1 Regression

(Cohn *et al.*, 1995) defined the principal of optimal active learning. In this definition optimal active learning is the method that asks the label of the example that retraining the predictive model with the provided label will result in the lowest expected error on the test set. The test error can be formulated as follows:

$$\int_x E_T[(\hat{y}(x;\mathcal{D}) - y(x))^2|x]P(x)dx \tag{4.1}$$

where $E_T[.]$ denotes expectation over $P(y|x)$ and over training data $\mathcal{D}^{\text{train}}$, and $P(x)$ is the marginal distribution of x. As $y(x)$ is not known in the training phase, it can be estimated by its expected value $E(\hat{y}(x))$ given the predictive models are unbiased. To compute the expected value, the predictive model must be able to provide $p(y|x)$. (Cohn *et al.*, 1995) applied this principal for two simple regression models, i.e. Locally Weighted Regression and Mixture of Gaussian. Note that knowing $P(x)$ is the requirement of this approach.

(Cohn *et al.*, 1995) was one of the earliest work on active learning and influenced a lot this literature. It was later extended for other regression models (Sugiyama, 2006; Sugiyama & Rubens, 2008). The principle of optimal active learning introduced in this paper is not limited to regression task and can be also applied for classification problem. In the next section, we will review some of these works.

4.1.2 Classification

(Nicholas & McCallum, 2001) relaxed the constraint of the knowledge of $P(x)$ in Equation 4.1 by estimating it based on the pool data. They describe their method in the framework of binary classification and used naive Bayes classifier because it is efficient for incremental learning. The algorithm of (Nicholas & McCallum, 2001) is explained in Algorithm 3. The drawback of this method is that it is expensive in terms of time especially when the size of the pool data is large. Moreover, estimating $P(x)$ from the pool data might be inaccurate.

Algorithm 3 The algorithm of (Nicholas & McCallum, 2001)

Input: $\mathcal{D}^{label}$, $\mathcal{D}^{pool}$, $\hat{f}$
Output: D^{query}

1. train the classifier $\hat{f}$ using the current labeled examples $\mathcal{D}^{label}$
   (a) consider each unlabeled example, x, in the pool $\mathcal{D}^{pool}$ as a candidate for the next labeling request
      i. consider each possible label, y, for x, and add the pair (x, y) to the training set $\mathcal{D}^{label}$
      ii. re-train the classifier $\hat{f}$ with the enlarged training set, $\mathcal{D}^{pool} + (x, y)$
      iii. estimate the resulting expected loss as in Equation 4.2 or Equation 4.3
   (b) assign to x the average expected losses for each possible labeling, y, weighted according to the current classifiers posterior, $\hat{P}_{\mathcal{D}^{label}}(y|x)$
2. select for labeling the unlabeled example x that generated the lowest expected error on all other examples and add it to $\mathcal{D}^{query}$ and $\mathcal{D}^{label}$.

Given $\mathcal{D}^*$ is $\mathcal{D} + (x^*, y^*)$, the loss function is as follows:

$$\tilde{E}_{\hat{P}^*_{\mathcal{D}}} = \frac{1}{|\mathcal{D}^{\mathrm{pool}}|} \sum_{x \in \mathcal{D}^{\mathrm{pool}}} \sum_{y \in Y} \hat{P}_{\mathcal{D}^*}(y|x) \log(\hat{P}_{\mathcal{D}^*}(y|x)) \tag{4.2}$$

and for 0/1 loss:

$$\tilde{E}_{\hat{P}^*_{\mathcal{D}}} = \frac{1}{|\mathcal{D}^{\text{pool}}|} \sum_{x \in \mathcal{D}^{\text{pool}}} \left(1 - \underset{y \in Y}{\text{argmax}} \, \hat{P}_{\mathcal{D}^*}(y|x) \right) \tag{4.3}$$

(Nguyen & Smeulders, 2004) takes another approach to approximate the principal of optimal active learning. Equation 4.1 shows that the data uncertainty should be weighted with the prior density $P(x)$. In (Nguyen & Smeulders, 2004), $P(x)$ is approximated via clustering, which can be done offline without the interaction with human. Therefore, we need a selection criterion that gives priority to two types of samples: samples close to the classification boundary and samples that are cluster representatives. The combination of two criteria acts like a soft AND, which is formalized as follows:

$$x^* = \underset{x \in \mathcal{D}^{pool}}{\text{argmax}} (1 - |f(x)| p(x)$$

where $|f(x)|$ is the distance of example x to the decision boundary f and $P(x)$ is the probability that x is a representative of a cluster.

(Baram *et al.*, 2004) proposed a framework based on multi-armed bandit algorithm (Sutton & Barto, 1998a) to combine several active learning algorithms. The idea behind this framework is that the best active learning algorithm depends on the dataset and should be determined at run time. In this framework all active learning algorithms have chances to select queries. After each query and updating the predictive model, the probability of the active learning algorithm that selected the query is changed based on the gained improvement in the classifier. More improvement indicates the suitability of the algorithm and increases the probability and vice versa. To evaluate the proposed framework, (Baram *et al.*, 2004) use three active learning methods. The first method that is called SIMPLE selects examples that are close to decision boundary because they pose higher uncertainty for the model (Tong & Koller, 2002). In contrast, the second method chooses examples that are far from the decision boundary. It is called Kernel Farthest-First (KFF) (Baram *et al.*, 2004). Finally, the third method is (Nicholas & McCallum, 2001), which was already explained. All three methods use SVM as the predictive model.

(Osugi *et al.*, 2005) proposed a lighter version of (Baram *et al.*, 2004) that includes only two active learning methods. One method for exploitation (SIMPLE) and the one method for exploration (KFF). The details of (Osugi *et al.*, 2005) is explained in Algorithm 4. First the model is trained using the initial training data $\mathcal{D}$. Then the algorithm flips a biased coin with probability p of coming up heads. If the outcome is heads, it means the exploration method (KFF) should be executed. Otherwise, the next example is chosen with SIMPLE to exploit the current decision boundary. After training using this new example, a new hypothesis $\hat{f}'$ is computed ($\hat{f}$ is the hypothesis before asking the label of the new example). To determine whether the exploration was successful, the predictions of $\hat{f}$ and $\hat{f}'$ are compared to see how much they differ. The change is denoted by $d(\hat{f}, \hat{f}') \in [-1, +1]$. If $d(\hat{f}, \hat{f}')$ is positive, it means that the changes are significant and the exploration was successful. Therefore we need to keep the probability p high to do more exploration. If $d(\hat{f}, \hat{f}')$ is negative, we reduce p to increase the chance of exploitation.

In Algorithm 4, ϵ is a parameter that specifies the upper- and lower-bounds of p (so there is always a chance of exploring and exploiting). Also λ is a learning rate for updating p . The similarity function $s_1(\hat{f}, \hat{f}\prime)$ computes the normalized cosine similarity between the old predictions $(\hat{f})$ and the new predictions $(\hat{f}')$. Although mathematically the minimum could be -1, practically in the experiments it is not smaller that 1/2. Therefore, the computed similarity is mapped to the range of $[-1, 1]$ by function d. The larger the value of d, the higher the probability of exploration in the next query.

(Poupart, March 2009) proposed a general idea on applying Reinforcement Learning (RL) for active learning problem. The idea explicitly models the sequence of queries with a Markov Decision Process (MDP) and learns the best sequence of queries with RL. The speaker did not do any experiment in this regard and suggested to apply it for realistic assistive technology (Ibbme *et al.*, 2005). In order to apply this idea to the pool-based active learning problem, one should define state, action, and a reward function according to the characteristics of active learning which is non-trivial.

4.2 Active Learning for Recommender Systems

The literature of active learning for recommender systems has been evolved according to the progress made in recommendation technique algorithms. There is no active learning method for early recommendation techniques which were not based on collaborative filtering. After introducing Nearest Neighbor (NN) (Konstan *et al.*, 1997b) as the first collaborative filtering technique, active learning methods were also developed based on NN (Kohrs & Merialdo, 2001; Rashid *et al.*, 2002). Interestingly, that the authors do not call their method active learning. They aim to develop criteria in a way that with minimum questions maximum information about new user preferences is gained. Basically, this is what active learning does in machine learning. Therefore, we consider those works and other similar works part of the literature of active learning for recommender systems.

4.2.1 Nearest Neighbor

Active learning, in the context of the new user problem, was introduced by (Kohrs & Merialdo, 2001). They studied two methods to find items for querying from new users. The methods are based on statistics collected from ratings of training users to items.

Algorithm 4 The algorithm of (Osugi *et al.*, 2005)

Input: $\mathcal{D}^{label}$, $\mathcal{D}^{pool}$, $\hat{f}$, F
Output: $\mathcal{D}^{\hat{query}}$

$$\begin{aligned} \sigma_1 : X \times Y^X &\longmapsto \mathbb{R} && (\textit{SVM Simple as exploitation algorithm}) \\ (x, \hat{f}) &\longmapsto \sigma(x, \hat{f}) \end{aligned}$$

$$\begin{aligned} \sigma_2 : X \times Y^X &\longmapsto \mathbb{R} && (\textit{KFF as exploration algorithm }) \\ (x, \hat{f}) &\longmapsto \sigma(x, \hat{f}) \end{aligned}$$

Train $\hat{f}$ on $\mathcal{D}^{label}$: $\hat{f} := F(\mathcal{D}^{label})$
$\mathcal{D}^{query} := \emptyset$
$p := \textit{initial value}$
$S = \{x_1, x_2, ..., x_m\} = \mathcal{D}^{pool} \dot{\cup} \mathcal{D}^{label}$
for $i = 1$ to N **do**
  $a = U(0{,}1)$ (*A random number between* 0 *to* 1)
  if $(a < p)$ (exploration)
    $x^* := \text{argmax}_{x \in \mathcal{D}^{pool}}\ \sigma_2(x^*, \hat{f})$
    remove x^* from $\mathcal{D}^{pool}$
    Query y from Oracle : $y := f(x^*)$ (label of x^*)
    $\mathcal{D}^{query} := \mathcal{D}^{query} \dot{\cup} \{(x^*, y)\}$
    $\hat{f} = (\hat{f}(x_1), \hat{f}(x_2), ..., \hat{f}_1(x_m))$
    $\hat{f}\prime := F(\mathcal{D}^{label} \dot{\cup} \mathcal{D}^{query})$
    $\hat{f}\prime = (\hat{f}\prime(x_1), \hat{f}\prime(x_2), ..., \hat{f}\prime(x_m))$
    $s_1(\hat{f}, \hat{f}\prime) = \frac{<\hat{f}, \hat{f}\prime>}{||\hat{f}|| \, ||\hat{f}\prime||}$
    $d(\hat{f}, \hat{f}\prime) = 3 - 4 s_1(\hat{f}, \hat{f}\prime)$
    $p = max(min(p\lambda exp(d(\hat{f}, \hat{f}\prime)), 1 - \epsilon), \epsilon)$
  else (exploitation)
    $x^* := \text{argmax}_{x \in \mathcal{D}^{pool}}\ \sigma_1(x, \hat{f})$
    remove x^* from $\mathcal{D}^{pool}$
    Query y from Oracle : $y := f(x^*)$ (label of x^*)
    $\mathcal{D}^{query} := \mathcal{D}^{query} \dot{\cup} \{(x^*, y)\}$
    $\hat{f} := F(\mathcal{D}^{label} \dot{\cup} \mathcal{D}^{query})$
end for

The first method measures the variance of ratings of each item as follows:

$$var_i = \frac{\sum_{u \in U_i} (r_{ui} - \bar{R}_i)^2}{|U_i|} \tag{4.4}$$

where U_i is the set of training users who have rated item i and $\bar{R}_i$ is the average ratings of item i. The items are sorted according to their variance descendingly and the top N items are selected for query.

The second method is aimed to find an item that when its ratings is known, it reveals the best user preferences. For that, the authors select items with the highest entropy in which the entropy is measured as follows:

$$ent_i = - \sum_{u \in U_i, r \in R} P(r|u,i).log(P(u|i,r)) \tag{4.5}$$

where $\mathcal{D}_i$ contains ratings for item i, $P(r|u,i)$ is the probability that user u rates item i with ratings r, and $P(u|i,r)$the probability that given the rating r has been observed for item i, the user is u.

(Rashid *et al.*, 2002) expanded (Kohrs & Merialdo, 2001) by using a number of strategies that are more suitable than variance or entropy:

- **Popularity**: Rank all items in descending order according to the number ratings.
- **Popularity*Entropy** : Rank items by the product of popularity and entropy.
- **Item-Item personalized** : Select items using any strategy until the user has given at least one rating. Then compute the similarity between the rated items and other items and select the item with the highest similarity. Update the list of similar items whenever the user provides more ratings.

The authors conduct their experiments on the MovieLens dataset. The results show that the item-item personalization performed the best in choosing items that users can rate, while Entropy was the worst. Also, in terms of the test error, Popularity*Entropy did best and Popularity was marginally behind it. Again, Entropy is the worst strategy. The reason of poor performance of Entropy is that this strategy selects items that users are less likely to have seen. With fewer training data, i.e rated items, the test error is also adversely affected.

Surprisingly, while the item-item personalization is able to receive the most number of ratings, its test error is even worse than the random selection strategy. The reason is that the item-item personalization selects items that system has already accurate predictions for them since the queried items are similar to items that have already been rated by the new user. Therefore, although the user gives rating to many queried items but the ratings are not very informative. In chapter 5, we will apply the most popular strategy in AM.

4.2.2 Aspect Model

In general, model-based collaborative filtering outperforms NN. Aspect Model (AM) is one of the earliest model-based collaborative filtering techniques. (Jin & Si, 2004) developed the first active learning for aspect model. In contrast to the papers that were introduced in section 4.2.1, (Jin & Si, 2004) explicitly call their work active learning because it has been inspired from a an existing active learning method for Bayesian networks (Tong & Koller, 2000a).

Active learning techniques usually select examples for querying that pose higher uncertainty for the model. One way to measure the uncertainty is entropy. Given aspect model as the recommendation model, active learning criterion based on entropy would be as follows:

$$i_u^* = \underset{i \in I}{\operatorname{argmin}} - \left\langle \sum_{f \in Z} \theta_{u_f|i,r} \log \theta_{u_f|i,r} \right\rangle_{P(r|u,i)} \tag{4.6}$$

where i_u^* is the best query for user u, and $\theta_{u_f|m,r}$ denotes the updated user parameters after retraining with the obtained rating r for item i. As the exact rating r is not known before query, its expected value is used. The expected value is computed based on the current model $P(r|u, m)$.

The drawback of this method is that it strictly categorizes users into one class. However, in the reality users may belong to more than one class. For example, both comic and action movies may be interesting for users. To eliminate this issue, (Jin & Si, 2004) developed a Bayesian selection approach. This method selects item i in a way that the updated user parameters $\theta_{u_f|i,r}$ will become closer to the true user parameters θ_u^{true}.

$$i_u^* = \underset{i \in I}{\operatorname{argmax}} \left\langle \sum_{f \in Z} \theta_{u_f}^{true} \log \frac{\theta_{u_f|i,r}}{\theta_{u_f}^{true}} \right\rangle_{P(r|u,i)} \tag{4.7}$$

As the true user parameters are not known upfront, they are estimated as the expectation over the posterior distribution of the user parameters. Computing the expectation is expense. Therefore, (Jin & Si, 2004) conduct their experiments on MovieRating and Each Movie, which are small datasets[1]. Running the Bayesian approach for large datasets like Netflix would be intractable.

The items selected by the Bayesian approach will improve the estimation of the user parameters provided the user is able to give a rating for the queried item. But the fact is that users do not know the ratings of all items. For example, users do not watch all movies, so they cannot rate them. Therefore, in addition to selecting the items that are informative, i.e will improve the accuracy of user parameters given user rates them, the active learning method should also take into account the probability that an

[1]Both datasets are not available for download any longer.

item will receive a rating from user. To address this point, (Harpale & Yang, 2008) extended (Jin & Si, 2004) and introduced an additional term $P(i|u)$ into Equation 4.7 that is the probability of getting a rating on item i from user u:

$$i_u^* = \tag{4.8}$$

$$\underset{i}{\operatorname{argmax}} \in I \left(\left\langle \sum_{f \in Z} \theta_{u_f}^{true} \log \frac{\theta_{u_f|i,r}}{\theta_{u_f}^{true}} \right\rangle_{P(r|u,i)} \right) P(i|u)$$

The multiplication of the Bayesian selection criterion from Equation 4.7 and the personalization term $P(i|u)$ acts as a soft-AND which is maximized when both the multiplicands are maximized. $P(i|u)$ is approximated as follows:

$$P(i|u) = \sum_{f \in Z} P(i|f)P(f|u) \tag{4.9}$$

$$P(i|f) = \frac{\sum_{u \in U} P(f|u)I(u,i)}{\sum_{u \in U} \sum_{i' \in I} P(f|u)I(u,i')} \tag{4.10}$$

$I(u,i) = 1$, if user has rated item i and 0 otherwise

The authors mention that the proposed approach can be applied to other types of recommendation model besides aspect model.

4.2.3 Decision Trees

The reason that we cannot use CF for new users is that CF algorithm computes recommendations for the target user based on the opinions of other users with similar taste,i.e neighbors. As the new user has not given any ratings, it is not possible to find her neighbors. (Rashid *et al.*, 2008) extended their own previous work (Rashid *et al.*, 2002) and proposed an innovative approach to deal with this problem. The idea is to interpret the new user preference elicitation process as the problem of finding the most similar neighbors for her. And it is done in two steps: first, it groups training users into clusters and then it finds the right cluster of the new user. The ratings of the users of the assigned cluster are used to predict ratings for the new user. In this way, the problem of lacking ratings for new users is solved. The use of ratings is to find the neighbor users, i.e the right cluster of the target users. However, the problem is not as easy as it seems! There are two major questions:

- How to cluster training users?
- How to find the right cluster of the new user?

To answer the first question, (Rashid *et al.*, 2008) uses an arbitrary clustering technique. The goal of clustering is to partition objects in such a way that the similarities of the objects in clusters are maximized, and the similarities of the objects between clusters are minimized. Therefore, if the same similarity measure is used both to find neighbors in CF and to find clusters, a user cluster can be considered as a user neighborhood.

For the second question, (Rashid *et al.*, 2008) leverages decision trees to classify training users. In decision trees, the input variables are the items and the possible values are the ratings. After building decision trees, they are used for interviewing new users. First the new user is at the root of the tree. The item that was already used to split the root node is selected as the first query. Depending on the new user's answer to the queried item, she moves to one of the child nodes. Then the second item is queried. The second item is the item that splits the child node. This process continues until specific number of queries. As one can see, the best item to split a node in decision trees is also the best item to query from the new user. The reason is that the split item leads to the most coherent clusters, which is also the aim of CF.

Unfortunately, this ideal decision tree solution may not be possible because of two reasons:

- **Missing ratings:** Users usually rate only a small portion of items. Therefore, there are many missing ratings in recommender systems datasets. This, won't let us to build decision trees.
- **Multiple cluster:** Users may belong to more than one cluster, but decision trees push users into one node.

Due to the above issues, (Rashid *et al.*, 2008) makes two simplifications. First, it does not build complete decision trees. It means no classification is done. Second, instead of building decision trees using ID3 or similar algorithms, (Rashid *et al.*, 2008) define a new criterion, which is called IGCN (Information Gain through Clustered Neighbors) :

$$IG(i) = H(C) - \sum_{r} \frac{|C_i^r|}{|C|} H(C_i^r) \tag{4.11}$$

where $H(C)$ denotes the entropy of the current node, $|C|$ is the number of users in the current node (cluster), $|C_i^r|$ is the number of users who have rated item i with rating r, and $H(C_i^r)$ is the entropy in the corresponding cluster. Intuitively, this criterion seeks items that will cluster training users in the most coherent manner. Remember this is the principal of CF. To measure the coherence in a cluster, entropy is used. The more the similarity among users in a cluster, the less the entropy. The entropy of the child nodes are weighted according to the number of users in the cluster and total number of users $\frac{|C_i^r|}{|C|}$. The weighted summation is subtracted from the current entropy to produce the Information Gain (IG). The best item is the one that has the highest IG.

The main aspect of (Rashid *et al.*, 2008) is that the interview process is adaptive (personalized). It means new users receive different queries according to their responses to the previous queries. In contrast, static approaches present the same items to all users, regardless of how they rate the queried items. But it would be more clever if system exploits the growing knowledge of the user being interviewed.
(Golbandi *et al.*, 2011) improved (Rashid *et al.*, 2008) in two ways:

- The classification stage is removed
- The clustering is done according to CF objective function

Here, each interior node is labeled with an item $i \in I$ and each edge with the user's response to item i. The new user preference elicitation corresponds to following a path starting at the root by asking the user to rate items associated with the tree nodes along the path and traversing the edges labeled by the users response until a leaf node is reached. Here, decision trees are ternary. Each internal tree node represents a single item on which the user is queried. After answering the query, the user proceeds to one of the three subtrees, according to her answer. The answer is either Like, Dislike, or Unknown.

Each tree node represents a group of users and predicts item ratings by taking the average of ratings among corresponding users. Formally, let t be a tree node and $U_t \subseteq U$ be its associated set of users. $\mathcal{D}^t$ denotes a subset of $\mathcal{D}^{\text{train}}$, which belong to the node t:

$$\mathcal{D}^t := \{(u, i, r) \in U \times I \times R \mid u \in U_t\},$$

the profile of the item i in the node t is denoted as $\mathcal{D}_i^t$:

$$\mathcal{D}_i^t := \{(u, r) \in U \times R \mid u \in U_t\},$$

The predicted rating of item i at the node t is:

$$\hat{r}_{ti} = \frac{\sum\limits_{(u,r)\in\mathcal{D}_i^t} r_{ui} + \lambda_1 \hat{r}_{si}}{|\mathcal{D}_i^t| + \lambda_1} \tag{4.12}$$

To avoid over-fitting, the prediction of the item i is regularized towards its prediction in the parent node r_{si}. λ_1 is the regularization factor. The effect of the regularization for the item i becomes more significant when the number of the ratings in the item profile $\mathcal{D}_i^t$ is less. The squared error associated with node t and item i is: $(e_i^t)^2 = \sum\limits_{(u,r)\in D_i^t} (r - \hat{r}_{ti})^2$.
Also, the overall squared error at node t is: $(e^t)^2 = \sum\limits_{i\in I} (e_i^t)^2$.

Building decision trees is done in a top-down manner. For each internal node the best splitting item is the one that divides the users into three groups such that the total squared prediction error is minimized. This process continues recursively with each of the subtrees and at the end all users are partitioned among subtrees.

Suppose we are at node t. Per each candidate item i, three candidate child nodes are defined: $tL(i)$, $tD(i)$, $tU(i)$ representing users who like the item i, dislike it, and have not rated it respectively. The squared error associated with this item is $Err_t(i) = (e^{tL})^2 + (e^{tD})^2 + (e^{tU})^2$. Among all candidate items, the item that minimizes the following equation is the best :

$$splitter(t) = \underset{i \in I}{\text{argmin}}\ Err_t(i) \tag{4.13}$$

Note that the way decision trees have been used in (Golbandi *et al.*, 2011) poses some ambiguities. In chapter 7, we will address these ambiguities.

(Zhou *et al.*, 2011) modified (Golbandi *et al.*, 2011) by associating matrix factorization to decision trees. The idea is to parameterize user features to be a function of the responses to the possible queries of the interview process and use matrix factorization to compute the user features. To learn user and item features in MF, the following objective function is minimized:

$$(T, H) = \underset{T \in \mathcal{H}, H}{\text{argmin}} \sum_{(u,i,r) \in \mathcal{D}^{\text{train}}} (r - h_i^T T((\mathcal{D}_u^{\text{query}}))^2 + \lambda ||H||^2 \tag{4.14}$$

where $T(\mathcal{D}_u^{\text{query}})$ is a function that maps the responses of the user ($\mathcal{D}_u^{\text{query}}$) to user features $w_u \in \mathbb{R}^k$. Also, $\mathcal{H}$ is the space from which the function $T(\mathcal{D}_u^{\text{query}})$ is selected. The optimization is done through alternative optimization between the following two steps:

1. The item features are learned through a closed-form equation:

$$h_i = \left(\sum_{(u,i,r) \in \mathcal{D}^{\text{train}}} T(\mathcal{D}_u^{\text{query}}) T(\mathcal{D}_u^{\text{query}})^T + \lambda I \right)^{-1} \left(\sum_{(u,i,r) \in \mathcal{D}^{\text{train}}} r T(\mathcal{D}_u^{\text{query}}) \right) \tag{4.15}$$

2. Given h_i, a decision tree T is learned such that

$$T = \underset{T \in \mathcal{H}}{\text{argmin}} \sum_{(u,i,r) \in \mathcal{D}^{\text{train}}} (r - T(\mathcal{D}_u^{\text{query}})^T h_i)^2 \tag{4.16}$$

The decision tree is learned by finding the best split item at each node. The best split item is the one that meets the following objective function:

$$i^* = \underset{p \in I}{\text{argmin}} \sum_{(u,i,r) \in \mathcal{D}_p^{like}} (r - w_L^T h_i)^2 + \sum_{(u,i,r) \in \mathcal{D}_p^{dislike}} (r - w_D^T h_i)^2 + \sum_{(u,i,r) \in \mathcal{D}_p^{unk}} (r - w_U^T h_i)^2 \tag{4.17}$$

where $\mathcal{D}_p^{like}$, $\mathcal{D}_p^{dislike}$, and $\mathcal{D}_p^{unk}$ contains the ratings of users in the child nodes corresponds to the answers "Like", "Dislike", and "Unknown", respectively:

$$\mathcal{D}_p^{like} = \{(u,i,r) \in \mathcal{D}^{\text{train}} | u \in D_p, r > 3\}$$
$$\mathcal{D}_p^{dislike} = \{(u,i,r) \in \mathcal{D}^{\text{train}} | u \in D_p, r \leq 3\}$$
$$\mathcal{D}_p^{unk} = \{(u,i,r) \in \mathcal{D}^{\text{train}} | u \notin D_p\}$$

moreover, w_L, w_D, and w_U are the optimal user features in the child nodes corresponds to the answers of "Like", "Dislike" and "Unknown", respectively:

$$w_L = \underset{w}{\operatorname{argmin}} \sum_{(u,i,r)\in\mathcal{D}^{like}} (r - w^T h_i)^2$$
$$w_D = \underset{w}{\operatorname{argmin}} \sum_{(u,i,r)\in\mathcal{D}^{dislike}} (r - w^T h_i)^2$$
$$w_U = \underset{w}{\operatorname{argmin}} \sum_{(u,i,r)\in\mathcal{D}^{unk}} (r - w^T h_i)^2$$

The algorithm starts by random initialization of item features. Then, decision trees are built according to the Equation 4.17. After learning the tree, the item features are updated using the learned user features. This continues until the convergence is reached.

We believe that (Zhou *et al.*, 2011) is too expensive both in terms of time and memory. The computation complexity for constructing decision trees is $O(N \sum_{u\in U} |D_u|^2 + l|I|k^3 + l|I|^2k^2)$ where N is the depth of the tree, $|D_u|$ is the number of ratings by user u, l is the number of nodes, $|I|$ is the number of items, and k is the number of latent features (Zhou *et al.*, 2011). Imagine we are going to apply this method for the Netflix dataset. In this dataset, $\sum_{u\in U} |D_u|^2 \approx 6.48^{10}$, $|I| \approx 18$k, and let say $k = 50$. The number of nodes l is $\sum_{i=0}^{q} 3^i$, so let's say $q = 7$, then l would be 3280. Considering all these numbers and the complexity of (Zhou *et al.*, 2011), the total number of operations would be 3.4×10^{13}, which is really huge. In chapter 7, we will propose a new method (FDT), which for the same dataset, needs 4.58×10^9 operations meaning it is 7423 time faster than (Zhou *et al.*, 2011)!

The complexity becomes even larger when we note that in (Zhou *et al.*, 2011) decision trees are not built only once. After building decision trees in one iteration, item features are updated and again decision trees are built using the updated item features. And the loop continues until convergence is met. Although (Zhou *et al.*, 2011) conduct their experiments on the Netflix data set, unfortunately the authors do not report the running time of their algorithm. Moreover, in addition to the time complexity, the required memory to store decision trees is also large. We have to store user features of all nodes to update item features after building the tree.

The scalability becomes even more important when we notice that Netflix is not the larger datasets for recommendation problem. Yahoo Music[1] contains 717 M ratings, so it is more than 7 times bigger than Netflix. Therefore, we need to think about the scalability of our approaches. Otherwise, even active learning methods are accurate, it is not possible to apply them in big recommender systems, especially when we take into consideration how information overload is growing up every day.

[1] http://webscope.sandbox.yahoo.com/catalog.php?datatype=r

Chapter 5

Active Learning for Aspect Model

At the time we started this thesis, the state-of-the-art active learning method for recommender systems was based on Aspect Model (AM) (Jin & Si, 2004), which was later extended by (Harpale & Yang, 2008). As a result, we also decided to stick with the AM in the first step of my thesis and develop a new active learning method (Karimi *et al.*, 2011a). Note that AM was described in section 3 and (Harpale & Yang, 2008; Jin & Si, 2004) were explained in section 4.

5.1 Introduction

In chapters 3 and 4, we learned about many active learning criteria in machine learning. In this chapter, we want to take some inspiration from that literature and develop new criteria for active learning in the aspect model. But before that, we need to take into account two essential differences between active learning for classification (regression) and active learning for new user problems in recommender systems.

First, although there are no ratings for new users, an abundance of available ratings exists -collectively- from past users. We need to take advantage of such additional information. This point was not taken into account in (Jin & Si, 2004). They relied only on the ratings of new users to define uncertainty measures for items and eventually ended up with a complicated Bayesian method, which is very slow and intractable for new users of recommender systems.

The second difference is about the running time of active learning methods. New users play the role of the Oracle in recommender systems. In this context, there is an additional constraint that does not exist in machine learning. New users are not willing to be interrupted for so long to be queried. For example, we cannot ask them to wait 30 minutes until the recommender system finds the next query and ask them. As a result, active learning methods should be fast. Otherwise, even if they are, it is not possible to use them in real applications. (Jin & Si, 2004) suffers from this issue because it exploits a Bayesian which is very slow.

In the next section, we develop a fast active learning method which exploit the ratings of training users to find uncertain items for AM.

5.2 Informativeness in Aspect Model

In order to define an informativeness score based on the characteristics of AM, one needs to consider how ratings are predicted in AM. In AM, the unknown ratings are estimated according to Eqution 3.3. This equation consists of user-latent parameters and item-latent parameters. While the new users were being interviewed, we switched to online updating. Our motivation was to speed up the query selection step, which is crucial for new users as they are not willing to wait so long. In online updating, only the user parameters are updated, while the item parameters are not touched (Rendle & Schmidt-Thieme, 2008) because they have already been trained enough in the training phase of AM and adding only one more rating does not have a significant impact on them. Consequently, in order to improve the predictions for the new users, we should concentrate on the user parameters and find an item for updating the user parameters that would be effective to improve the parameters estimations when its rating is provided. In AM, the user parameters are learned as follows:

$$P(f|u) = \frac{\sum\limits_{\langle u',i,r\rangle:u'=u} P(f|u,r,i;\hat{\theta})}{\sum\limits_{f'} \sum\limits_{\langle u',i,r\rangle:u'=u} P(f'|u,r,i;\hat{\theta})} \tag{5.1}$$

where

$$P(f|u,r,i;\hat{\theta}) = \frac{\hat{p}(r|i,f)\hat{P}(f|u)}{\sum\limits_{f'} \hat{p}(r|i,f)\hat{P}(f'|u)} \tag{5.2}$$

$p(r|i,f)$ is a Gaussian distribution with mean $\mu_{i,f}$ and $\sigma_{i,f}$. Equation 5.2 shows that the user parameters depend on the item parameters. This dependence implies that accurate item parameters will result in accurate user parameters and vice versa. So, in order to find informative queries for the new users, we just need to find items with accurate parameters, since updating the new user parameters with the ratings of those items will consequently improve the new user parameters.

To find items with more accurate parameter estimations, we need to take into account how item parameters are learned in AM. In AM, there is a Gaussian distribution per each item. The distribution of the item i is learned using the ratings associated with the item i. From a statistical point of view, we know that one important factor in learning parameters is the number of samples (here samples mean ratings). The more the number samples, the better the estimation. Therefore, our proposed method selects *most popular* items since those items have many ratings and consequently, are more informative for the aspect model. We call our method as Most Popular for Aspect Model (MPAM). Another advantage of MPAM is that as the list of most popular items can be created beforehand, i.e before interviewing the new users, it is fast.

5.3 Comparing Aspect Model and Matrix Factorization

The performance of active learning techniques in recommender systems depends heavily on the recommendation model. The model influences the performance of active learning methods in two places. First, active learning criteria are defined based on the characteristics of the recommendation model. Second, the model should be updated after getting a new rating to produce new accuracy. Therefore, to develop a precise active learning method, we need to choose the right recommendation model. If the model is weak, the active learning method would also be inaccurate and vice versa.

In the previous section, we developed active learning based on AM. The motivation was that there were already two active learning methods based on AM. However, since the Netflix prize, MF has become very popular for recommender systems. Therefore, it is promising to develop active learning methods based on MF. In this section, we compare AM and MF to verify this hypothesis. The comparison is taking into account two factors: accuracy and time.

The training algorithm for AM is shown in Algorithm 5. This algorithm is based on Expected Maximization (EM) (Hastie *et al.*, 2001). The EM algorithm is an iterative method for finding the maximum likelihood of parameters in statistical models. The Algorithm 5 alternates between the expectation step (E-step) and the maximization step (M-step). In the E-step, we create a function for the expectation of the log-likelihood using the current estimate for user and item parameters. In the M-step, we compute the parameters that maximize the expected log-likelihood found in the E-step. When an epoch finishes, the user parameters are normalized so that $\sum_f p(f|u) = 1$ for each user u. Finally, the convergence criterion is checked and if it is met, the learning stops. The convergence happens if training error does not reduce any further or the number of iterations is larger than L.

According to the Algorithm 5, the time complexity of AM is $O(L \times |D| \times k)$. Interestingly, MF also has the same time complexity (Rendle & Schmidt-Thieme, 2008). However, despite the same complexity, MF needs less computations for two reasons:

1. The standard version of MF is an algebraic model, not a probabilistic model, so there is no need to normalize the user parameters after each iteration. The complexity of normalizing the users parameters is $O(L.|U|.k)$

2. The learning algorithm of MF is based on the Stochastic Gradient Descent (SGD). The SGD usually converges fast. So, although L is the same in MF and AM, in actual practice the effective number of iterations is lower in MF.

So far we have been discussing the training algorithm of MF and AM with all training data. In the case of online updating, the complexity of both models does not change. The only difference is that in online updating, $|D|$ is much smaller because it only contains the ratings of the new users.

Algorithm 5 The Learning Algorithm of Aspect Model (Hofmann, 2003)

Input: $\mathcal{D}^{\text{train}}$
Output: $p(f|u)$, $\mu_{i,f}$, and $\sigma_{i,f}$

```
loop {repeat until convergence}
  for r_ui in D^train do
    for f ← 1, ..., k do
      compute E-Step for f
    end for
    for f ← 1, ..., k do
      update p(f|u), μ_{i,f} , and σ_{i,f}
    end for
  end for
  for u ∈ U do
    for f ← 1, ..., k do
      normalize p(f|u)
    end for
  end for
  check the convergence
end loop
```

5.4 Experimental Result

5.4.1 Experimental Setup

We used MovieLens and MovieRating datasets in our experiments. The details of these datasets and the way they are split have already been described in chapter 2. The number of latent factors is 5 and 10 in MovieRating and MovieLens respectively according to (Jin & Si, 2004) and (Harpale & Yang, 2008). The Mean Absolute Error (MAE) is used to evaluate the performance of active learning algorithms, the same measure was used in (Jin & Si, 2004) and (Harpale & Yang, 2008). For each test user, the latent parameters are trained by 3 initial random ratings. After getting a new rating, the user parameters are retrained by online updating. Like (Jin & Si, 2004), it is assumed that new users are able to rate any queried item. As the baseline, we chose (Jin & Si, 2004) which is called Bayesian in this section. We implemented the baseline by ourself in Java. It should be mentioned that we calibrated our results against (Jin & Si, 2004) to ensure that our implementation is correct. We could reproduce the reported results of (Jin & Si, 2004) on the MovieRating datasets with a little error which is probably because of different splits.

First, we will report the results of active learning for AM. Next, we will compare AM and MF.

5.4.2 Result

The accuracy of MPAM, Bayesian and Random selection for MovieLens and MovieRating datasets is presented in Figure 5.1 and 5.4.2 respectively.

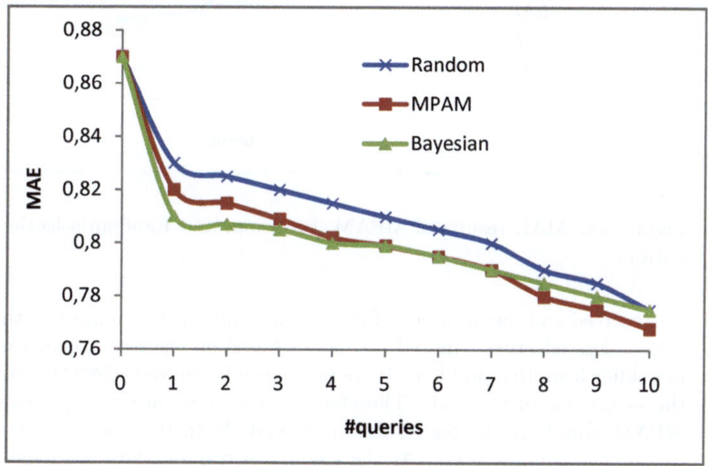

Figure 5.1: MAE results of MPAM, Bayesian, and Random selection in MovieLens dataset.

These charts can be divided into two parts: in the first part, the Bayesian method outperforms and in the second part, MPAM method overtakes the Bayesian method. Both methods aim to find an item that would improve the accuracy of new user parameters the most. But they have different approaches. The Bayesian method is personalized in the sense that new users receive different queries based on their user parameters. But MPAM is static and shows the same most popular queries to all users. In general, a personalized solution would be expected to give better results, as we see in the first part of the chart. However, it in the second part, the performance of the Bayesian slowly drops and finally converges to the random selection. The reason is that the Bayesian method is defined based on the new user parameters. The advantage of this approach is more obvious in the first queries, where the new user parameters are inaccurate. In this situation, the active learning criterion, which is defined based new user parameters, has a significant impact on the accuracy. However, as more ratings

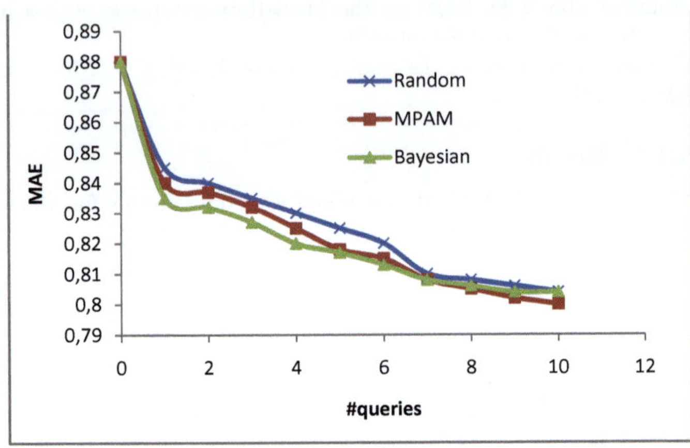

Figure 5.2: MAE results of MPAM, Bayesian, and Random selection in MovieRating dataset.

are received and the accuracy of the new user parameters improves, this criterion would also be less effective. But MPAM is not based on the new user parameters, so it does not suffer from this problem. Its performance has nevertheless the same tendency from the beginning to the end. Therefore, if new users are willing to answer 10 queries, MPAM would give better results in the end. Both Bayesian and the MPAM methods rely on the training users. As the amount of training data in MovieLens is larger, the difference between these methods and random is also more clear in this data set.

Now we will go on to compare the running time of MPAM against the running time of Bayesian. The running time means the time that new users have to wait to receive the next query, so we call it waiting time. The user waiting time of these methods, according to our experiments, is shown in Figure 5.3. The computation time of the MPAM method is much less than for the Bayesian method. It is because the Bayesian method needs a lot of computation for posterior estimation while MPAM incorporates the characteristics of the aspect model. This consideration provides a scalable method, the accuracy of which, however, is the same as the Bayesian method. Our initial goal was to develop a method that is scalable, though it is not more accurate than the Bayesian method. The results show that we have achieved even more than our goal because MPAM not only is more scalable than the Bayesian approach, it is also more accurate in the last queries. By considering both time and accuracy, the MPAM method is more suitable for the recommender system, especially as the size of the recommender system increases.

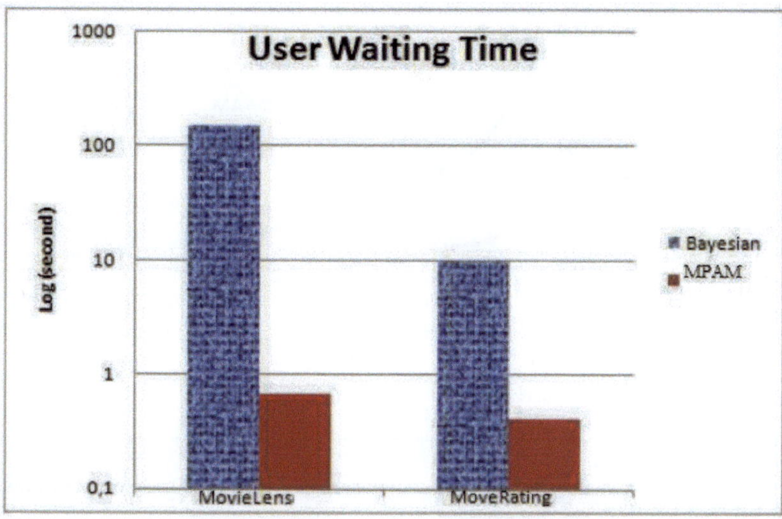

Figure 5.3: Average user waiting time in the MPAM and the Bayesian methods in MovieLens and MovieRating datasets. The axis y is log(seconds)

The last part of the experimental results deals with comparing AM and MF. In this part, we compare the accuracy of the active learning algorithm based on MF with the active learning algorithm based on AM. The objective is to show that MF is a better predictive model to be used for developing the active learning algorithm. For this reason, in order to have a fair comparison we focus only on the predictive model and simply apply the random selection of the queried items for both MF and AM. Figure 5.4 depicts the resulting MAE as a function of the number of queried items in the MovieLens dataset. MF outperforms AM, indicating its superiority as the predictive model for new user problems in recommender systems.

In addition to accuracy, applying active learning to new user problems in recommender systems requires a further criterion. The new user's preference elicitation is an interactive scenario and long time interruptions can cause the user to leave the conversation. As a result, the active learning method also has to be fast and not require long user waiting times, i.e. the time that the users wait before being asked a new query. As already mentioned, the retraining of MF and AM is done using online updating. The retraining time is equivalent to the time that the new user waits before being asked a new query (user waiting time). Table 5.1 compares the user waiting time in AM and MF. MF requires shorter user waiting times because it converges faster and needs less computations. Therefore, the superiority of MF in accuracy and time makes it an ideal backbone for active learning methods.

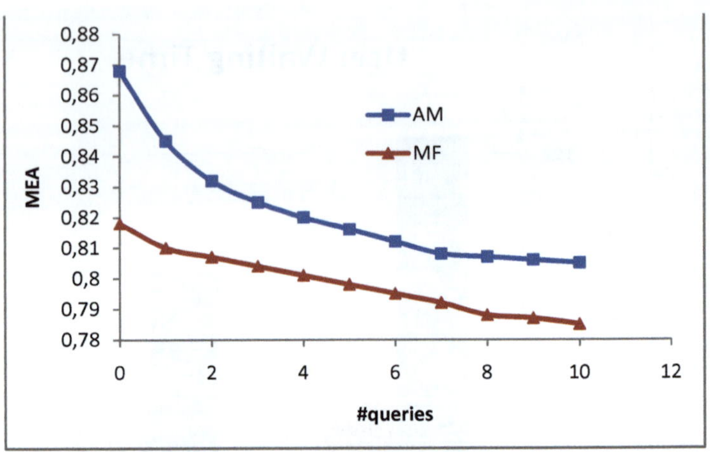

Figure 5.4: Active Learning trends for 10 active-iterations

Table 5.1: Average user waiting time in AM and MF (time in seconds)

	Aspect Model	Matrix Factorization
MovieLens	44.5	3.9
MovieRating	36.7	2.1

Both AM and MF are trained on the basis of 10 latent dimensions. In MF, the learning rate α is set to 0.01 when MF is trained with all training data $\mathcal{D}^{\text{train}}$. But for retraining, it is reduced to 0.001 because the number of the provided ratings of the new user is low and learning should be done more carefully.

5.5 Summary and Future Work

In this chapter, we developed a scalable active learning for AM in recommender systems. It opts for exploiting the learning algorithm of AM to find informative queries. Eventually, it concludes that the most popular items are more informative for AM because they are more effective to improve the accuracy of new user parameters. We compared our method (MPAM) to the state-of-the-art method (Jin & Si, 2004) on the basis of two factors: accuracy and running time. Nevertheless, the accuracy of the MPAM method is equal to, but the running time much faster than the baseline. The running time is a crucial factor for interviewing new users because they are not willing to be interrupted for a long time. Also, we compared AM and MF to find out which one is more suitable as the underlying model of active learning. The results shows that MF is more accurate. Also, MF is faster because it exploits SGD for learning the parameters but AM is based on EM. Therefore, it would be more clever if we developed active learning methods based on MF.

As the results show, working on AM is not promising, so it will not be wise to work on AM in the future. However, the main advantage of AM is that it is a probabilistic model. In general, as we reviewed in chapters 3 and 4, defining active learning criterion for a probabilistic model is more straightforward. This is because there is already a framework to give us an uncertainty measure for candidate items. Therefore, it would be interesting to work on probabilistic MF (Salakhutdinov & Mnih, 2008) and try to define uncertainty based on the characteristics of this model.

Chapter 6

Active Learning for Matrix Factorization

This chapter consists of two parts. In the first part, after being inspired by the literature on active learning for machine learning, we develop several active learning methods for Matrix Factorization (MF) (Karimi *et al.*, 2011b,c). As in active learning, it is assumed that the Oracle has full rationality and is always able to give labels for the queried instances, we too stick with this assumption and suppose that new users are always able to rate the queried items. In the second part, we relax this assumption and make the problem more realistic in a way that new users are allowed not to provide ratings to items (Karimi *et al.*, 2012a). In fact, the second part is the preliminary work for the next two chapters.

6.1 Uncertainty in Latent Space

In chapters 3 and 4 we reviewed a number of different definitions for uncertainty in active learning. Now our motivation is to extend those notations for MF. Interestingly, all the active learning methods based on uncertainty have been developed for the classification problem. But rating prediction in recommender systems is a regression problem and we cannot directly apply active learning methods in classification for a regression task. Nevertheless, in this section, we were inspired by the definition of uncertainty for the SVM classifier and develop a new uncertainty measure for MF.

In active learning for linear discriminant classifiers, such as SVM, the uncertainty of instances that are close to the decision boundary is higher than examples that are far from decision boundary (Figure 6.1). The reason is that if the current position of the decision boundary changes a little in the next step of active learning, the instances that are close to the decision boundary are affected most by this change, while instances that are further away are not affected (Schohn & Cohn, 2000). We cannot apply this approach to define uncertainty in MF because MF is not a binary classifier in recommender systems, but a regression model. However, we try to get our inspiration from this definition and come up with an uncertainty measure for MF.

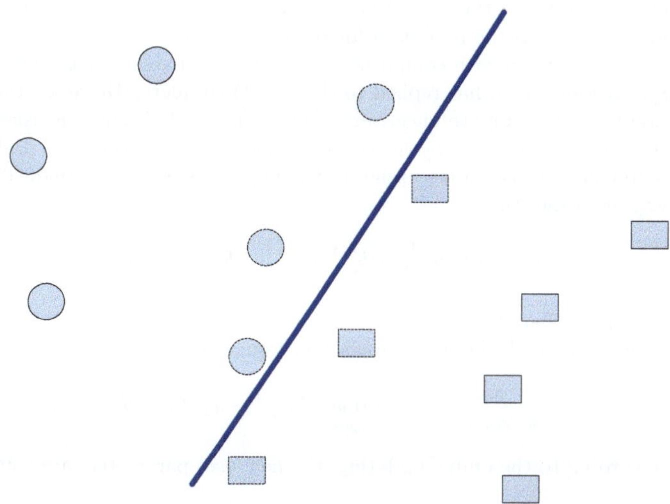

Figure 6.1: An example of active learning for binary classification in SVM classifier. Examples which are close to decision boundary pose higher uncertainty for the model. The uncertain examples are drawn with discreet lines.

To define the criterion of maximum uncertainty in the context of MF, we have to consider that user u, who has recently entered the recommender system, may have already provided only a small number of ratings. In this case, w_u in the latent space that MF creates is being computed based on inadequate information and, thus, the accuracy with which MF predicts ratings for u may be negatively impacted. The criterion to select the item, i^* , for which user u will be queried to provide a rating, is to determine the item that is most sensitive to the incorrect values of u's features in the latent space (w_u). Therefore, at the point when u has already replied to l queries, we compute predictions for each item i. The difference between the current predicted rating $\hat{r}^l_{ui}$ (i.e. after l queries) and the rating $\hat{r}^{l+1}_{ui}$ that will be predicted after u has replied to the $l+1$ query. This leads to the selection of the item i^* for the $l+1$ query, which is computed to have the maximum uncertainty based on Equation 6.1.

$$i^* = \underset{i \in D_u^{pool}}{\text{argmax}} \left| \hat{r}_i^{l+1} - \hat{r}_i^l \right| \tag{6.1}$$

where $\hat{r}^l$ ($\hat{r}^{l+1}$, respectively) is the predicted rating that MF predicts that user u will give for item i in the step after l ($l+1$, respectively) queries have been replied to by u. Also D_u^{pool} is the pool data for the new user u.

The problem with computing i^* based on Equation 6.1 is that we cannot compute $\hat{r}_{ui}^{l+1}$ before user u has replied to the $(l+1)$-th query. However, the purpose of Equation 6.1 is to compute uncertainty before the $l+1$-th query is asked in order to select the item to be queried by the $(l+1)$-th query. To overcome this problem, our approach is to consider the online updating technique (Rendle & Schmidt-Thieme, 2008). This way, it follows that:

$$i^* = \underset{i \in D_u^{pool}}{\operatorname{argmax}} \left| \mu + b_i^{l+1} + b_u^{l+1} + h_i^T w_u^{l+1} - \mu - b_i^l - b_u^l - h_i^T w_u^l \right| \tag{6.2}$$

Assuming that the item bias does not change during the active learning process and, with a simple algebraic manipulation, Equation 6.3 becomes:

$$i^* = \underset{i \in D_u^{pool}}{\operatorname{argmax}} \left| (w_u^{l+1} - w_u^l) h_i^T + b_u^{l+1} - b_u^l \right| \tag{6.3}$$

According to the online updating, the new user parameters are computed as follows:

$$w_{uf}^{l+1} = w_{uf}^l - \alpha \frac{\partial}{\partial w_{uf}} Opt(\mathcal{D}_u, W, H) \tag{6.4}$$

where D_u is the training set of new user u. In the same way, the new user bias is computed:

$$b_{uf}^{l+1} = b_{uf}^l - \alpha \frac{\partial}{\partial (w_{uf}, h_{if})} Opt(\mathcal{D}_u, W, H) \tag{6.5}$$

According to Equation 6.4 and 6.5 showing how w^{l+1} and b^{l+1} are computed respectively, we will have:

$$i^* = \underset{i \in \mathcal{D}_u^{pool}}{\operatorname{argmax}} \left| (-\alpha \frac{\partial}{\partial w_{uf}} Opt(\mathcal{D}_u, W, H)) h_i^T - \alpha \frac{\partial}{\partial (w_{uf}, h_{if})} Opt(\mathcal{D}_u, W, H) \right| \tag{6.6}$$

Now we need to compute two gradients, one to obtain the new user parameters w^{l+1} and one to obtain the new user bias b^{l+1}. For the new user parameters w^{l+1}, the gradient of the objective function is computed with respect to the item parameters h_i. But for the new user bias, the gradient is computed with respect to both user and item parameters (Koren, 2008). Formally, it means:

$$\frac{\partial}{\partial w_{uf}} Opt(D_u, W, H) = 2(\hat{r}_{ui} - r_{ui}) h_{if} \tag{6.7}$$

and

$$\frac{\partial}{\partial(w_{uf}, w_{uf})} Opt(D_u, W, H) = 2(\hat{r}_{ui} - r_{ui}) \tag{6.8}$$

The only difference between these two derivations is that in $\frac{\partial}{\partial(w_{u,f}, w_{u,f})} Opt(D_u, W, H)$, the item parameters disappear. Considering this fact and with a simple algebraic manipulation, Equation 6.6 becomes:

$$i^* = \underset{i \in D_u^{pool}}{\operatorname{argmax}} \left| (-\alpha \frac{\partial}{\partial(w_{uf}, h_{if})} Opt(D_u, W, H))(\|h_i^T\|^2 + 1) \right| \tag{6.9}$$

as α is constant for all candidate items i, we can drop it:

$$i^* = \underset{i \in D_u^{pool}}{\operatorname{argmax}} \left| \frac{\partial}{\partial(w_{uf}, h_{if})} Opt(D_u, W, H)(\|h_i^T\|^2 + 1) \right| \tag{6.10}$$

Finding $\frac{\partial}{\partial(w_{uf}, h_{if})} Opt(D_u, W, H)$ requires to know the actual rating r_{ui} to compute the test error $\hat{r}_{ui} - r_{ui}$, a fact that is not possible. To overcome this problem, we approximate an upper-bound for the test error by substituting r_{ui} with $r_{\max}$, which results in a conservative approximation regarding test error.

It is worthwhile to qualitatively analyze the resulting Equation 6.10. There are two factors in this equation: a) the gradient and b) the norm of item parameters. In order to understand why the gradient is important, the optimization procedure of MF should be taken into account. In MF, the stochastic gradient descent is usually used to optimize Equation 3.9 (Koren *et al.*, 2009). As the item parameters during the active learning process are fixed, this results in a convex optimization task. After getting a new rating from the new user, the corresponding user parameters are updated. The goal is to improve the estimation of the new user parameters with additional ratings. Therefore, active learning should select an item that improves the estimation of the user parameters more than other items. As the current user parameters are trained using only a few ratings, they are far from their accurate values. Therefore, they should be changed significantly. The only way to change them significantly is to maximize the gradient. Therefore, the item that changes the gradient as much as possible, may be also expected to improve the user parameters as much as possible. In fact, this heuristic is similar the "expected model change" criterion in active learning, which we mentioned in the chapter 3.

The second factor is the norm of the item parameters. Items with large norm are far away from the center and thus far from other items in the latent space that MF creates. Such far away items can be considered as outliers. These items are more informative, since they are different from ordinary items.

6.2 Uncertainty in Rating Space

There is an essential difference between active learning for classification (regression) and active learning for new user problems in recommender systems. Although there are no ratings for new users, an abundance of available ratings exist - collectively - from past users. In this section, we take advantage of such additional information and define a new criterion for uncertainty in recommender systems. The criterion is independent of the recommendation model and relies on the rating matrix. However, we will use MF for rating predictions.

Algorithm 6 Active Learning based on uncertainty in the rating matrix

Input : Number of queries (N), MF model
Output : Updated MF model

1: Predict the ratings for all items i using the item average method ($\bar{R}_i$)
2: **loop** {repeats until N questions}
3: Predict the ratings of the new user u for all candidate items i using MF ($\hat{r}_{ui}$)
4: For all candidate items, compute the difference between the predicted rating by MF and the item average ($\bar{R}_i - \hat{r}_i$)
5: select the item with the maximum difference
6: Ask the query
7: Retrain the model with the given rating
8: **end loop**

Algorithm 6 describes the proposed criterion. First, using the ratings of training users, the proposed criterion predicts the ratings of each item for the new user by the item average method. $\bar{R}_i$ denotes the item average for item i. As these predictions do not depend on the MF, they can be computed once for all items before starting to query new users. The item average prediction roughly tell us what to expect as predictions for new users. We also compute predictions for new users using MF. As new user parameters have been trained with just a few ratings, they are inaccurate, and consequently, the predictions are inaccurate, too. So we are uncertain about the MF predictions. The amount of uncertainty depends on the difference between the predicted rating using MF and the predicted rating using the item average. The bigger the difference, the greater the uncertainty. Therefore, the selection function would be as follows:

$$i^* = \underset{i \in D_u^{pool}}{\operatorname{argmax}} (\bar{R}_i - \hat{r}_i) \tag{6.11}$$

Note that in the Equation 6.11, we subtract $\hat{r}_i$ from $\bar{R}_i$. The other way around did not work in our experiments for MF. Perhaps it is because to compute the gradient of MF, we subtracted the actual rating from the predicted rating, i.e. ($\hat{r}_{ui} - r_{ui}$).

6.3 Non-myopic Active Learning

In this section, we develop a non-myopic active learning for MF. In contrast to myopic methods that aim to find the best *next* query, in the non-myopic approach the objective is to find the best *sequence* of queries. The major consequence of this difference is that non-myopic active learning may choose an example that is not the best next query, but considering the next queries, the sequence of all queries is optimal. This idea has been inspired by (Osugi *et al.*, 2005), where they develop non-myopic active learning for SVM. (Osugi *et al.*, 2005) consists of two algorithms: exploration and exploitation. The exploration algorithm selects examples far from decision boundary and the exploitation algorithms chooses examples close to decision boundary.

Non-myopic active learning considers the new user problem in recommender systems as an optimization task. The goal of this optimization task is to learn the new user preferences by querying them on the most informative items. The exploration-exploitation dilemma is a typical framework to address such problems. First, it explores the latent space to get closer to the optimal new user parameters. The optimal new user parameters ideally show the influence of factors on user preferences. Then, it exploits the learned parameters and slightly adjusts them. Both exploration and exploitation algorithms rely on the online updating (Rendle & Schmidt-Thieme, 2008) of MF, which was explained in section 3.2.4.

The exploration and exploitation algorithms are described in the following sections. Then, the solution for combining them into one method will be explained.

6.3.1 Exploration Algorithm

In chapter 3, we discussed that one criterion expected for active learning is model change. It selects the query that changes the model parameters as much as possible if we knew its label. As the initial model parameters are inaccurate, the query that changes the parameters as much as possible, will hopefully make them more accurate. The exploration algorithm is based on this criterion. As the new user parameters are computed with a few ratings, they are inaccurate and significantly different from the optimal parameters[1]. Therefore, in order to improve accuracy, we have to drastically change them. This is called exploration (Figure 6.2).

The exploration algorithm aims to select an item so that retraining the user parameters with the provided rating will change them as much as possible. To find such a query, we need to take into account how they are computed. In online updating, the user parameters are computed as follows (Rendle & Schmidt-Thieme, 2008):

$$w_{uf} \leftarrow w_{uf} - \alpha \frac{\partial}{\partial w_{uf}} Opt(r_{ui}, W, H) \tag{6.12}$$

[1]That is why active learning is used to getting additional ratings from the new user.

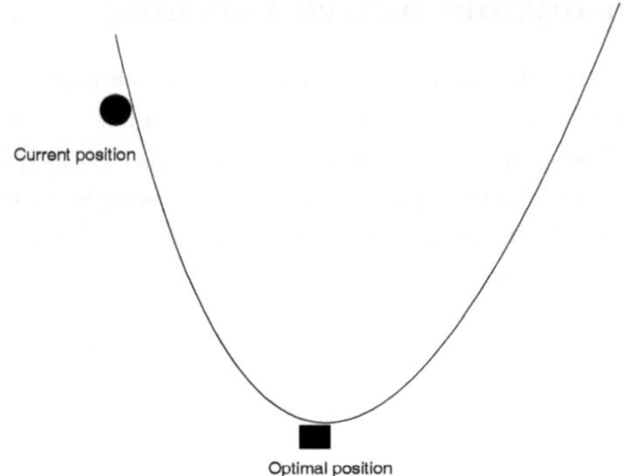

Figure 6.2: At the beginning of active learning, the new user parameters are inaccurate and far away from their optimal position in the latent space. To decrease the test error, we need to change the current position substantially to make it closer to the optimal position.

Clearly, the user parameters change as much as possible when the gradient is maximum. Therefore, we need to find an item which retraining the model with the provided rating will lead to maximum change in the gradient. The gradient is proportional to the product of item parameters in the latent space and the difference between the predicted rating and the true rating (prediction error) (Rendle & Schmidt-Thieme, 2008):

$$\frac{\partial Opt(\{r_{ui}\}, W, H)}{\partial w_{uf}} \propto (\hat{r}_{ui} - r_{ui}) \cdot h_{if} \tag{6.13}$$

Therefore, we need to choose an item that has a large prediction error or large parameters norm. In the experiments, we found that the prediction error dominated the norm of item parameters because the scale of the error was much larger than the item parameters norm. For this reason, we rely on the prediction error to maximize the gradient.

As the true rating is unknown, it is not possible to compute the prediction error. However, we already know that most of the ratings in the datasets like the MovieLens and Netflix are higher than 3 because users usually provide ratings for movies that they like. Therefore, it is expected that the prediction error would be large for items with small predicted ratings since the actual ratings are likely to be different from the predicted ratings. Therefore, the exploration algorithm selects items with the smallest predicted rating. We call this method MinRating. In the experiments, we will show that, in order to increase the gradient, MinRating works better compared to the method that selects items with large parameters norm (MaxNorm).

6.3.2 Exploitation Algorithm

So far, we were exploring the latent space by selecting an item that brings maximum change to the new user parameters. This is a good strategy in the first queries because, as we already mentioned, the user parameters are not accurate. However, as the new user parameters are retrained with more ratings, the accuracy of the estimated parameters also improves. Therefore, it is not necessary to change the user parameters significantly. Instead, the amount of change should be decreased so the user parameters are slightly adjusted to the optimal parameters (Figure 6.3). Again, based on the Equation 6.13, there is minimum change in the new user parameters when the gradient is minimum.

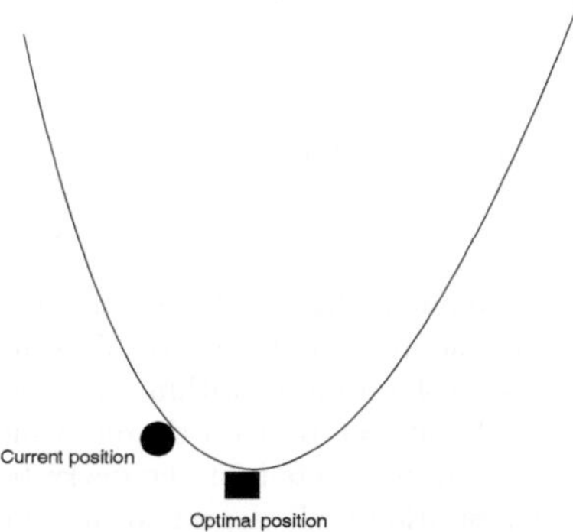

Figure 6.3: After a few queries, the user parameters get closer to the optimal parameter. In this situation, the parameters must be slightly changed to tune them towards the optimal parameters.

In order to minimize the gradient, the prediction error and item parameters should be minimized. As the value of the prediction error is larger, it makes sense to focus on the part similar to the situation where the goal was to maximize the gradient. This means selecting the item with the largest predicted rating. Hopefully, the actual rating will also be large and consequently the prediction error will also be small. However, this is not a good strategy because if the actual rating is not as large as the predicted rating, the prediction error will be large. This increases the gradient and consequently the changes of the user parameters. A safer strategy is to focus on the item parameters and minimize them. The values of the item parameters are already known and it is possible to select the item with the smallest latent parameters. As the gradient is the multiplication of the prediction error and the item parameters, if the item parameters are close enough to zero, it neutralizes the large value of the prediction error. Therefore, the gradient does not change significantly. We use the Euclidean norm of item parameters to determine how small the item parameters are. This method is called MinNorm.

6.3.3 Combining Exploration and Exploitation Algorithms

Now we have to come up with a solution to combine exploration and exploitation algorithms. The solution should be designed to pay more attention to exploration in the first queries and as the user provides more ratings, the weight of exploitation increases. The proposed method does the trade-off between exploration and exploitation by making two ranking lists. In the first list, the items are ranked based on the predicted ratings. The smaller the ratings, the lower the ranking. And in the second list, the items are ranked based on the norm of parameters. The smaller the norm, the lower the rank. Finally, the total rank of item i is computed as follows:

$$total\_rank(i) = rating\_rank(i) \cdot (1 - w) + norm\_rank(i) \cdot w \tag{6.14}$$

where w is the wight of exploitation :

$$w = query/N \tag{6.15}$$

where N is the maximum number of allowed queries and $query$ is the number of queried items so far. Before the first query, w is 0. This means that the first selected item is always based on the exploration algorithm. As more ratings are provided by the new user, the effect of exploitation is to select the query increases. In each step, the item with the minimum total rank is selected for the query because it satisfies both criteria for exploration and exploitation with respect to their importance. The reason for ranking items according to the predicted rating and the norm of item parameters is that the ranges of these two variables are different, so if we directly sum over the values, the predicted rating will dominate the norm of item parameters.

Non-myopic active learning is described in algorithm 7. Note that after each query, we have to update the list, which sorts items based on the rating predictions because the predictions change after retraining MF. But the list that sorts items based on the norm of item parameters is fixed during the active learning process because item parameters are fixed.

6.4 Optimal Active Learning

In chapter 4, we introduced the principle of optimal active learning. (Cohn *et al.*, 1995) applied this principle for two regression models and given some assumptions, they reached a closed-form formula. In this chapter, we aim to apply this principle to MF. Like (Cohn *et al.*, 1995) we also rely on some simplifications to cope with the difficulties we face in our approach. But those simplifications do not invalidate the approach of applying the principle of optimal active learning in MF.

Algorithm 7 Non-myopic Active Learning

Input : Number of queries (N), MF model
Output : Updated MF model

```
Sort items according to the item parameters norm and store them in list1
Sort items according to the predicted ratings and store them in list2
query = 0
w = query/N
loop {repeats until N questions}
   a=U(0,1)        A random number between 0 and 1
   if (a < w) then
      exploit
   else
      explore
   end if
   Ask the query
   Retrain the model with the given rating
   Update list2 according to the new predictions
   query = query + 1
   w = query/N
end loop
```

The aim of active learning is to improve the accuracy of the predictive model on the basis of test data. Therefore, the best strategy is to select a query that directly optimizes the expected error for the test data. This approach is applicable for predictive models in which this question can be answered in closed-form (Cohn *et al.*, 1995). Unfortunately, there are many tasks and models for which the optimal selection cannot be found efficiently in closed-form. Therefore, most of the active learning methods optimize different, non-optimal criteria, such as uncertainty (Schohn & Cohn, 2000). Nevertheless, in the following we exploit the characteristics of matrix factorization, which leads to a closed-form solution (see Proposition 1) and after being inspired by (Cohn *et al.*, 1995) develop a method that approximates the optimal solution.

As the optimization of accuracy requires the definition of an error measure, we adopt for this purpose one of the most commonly applied error measures in recommender systems, which is the Mean Absolute Error (MAE), which was explained in section 2.3.

Proposition 1. *The optimal selection of the queried item for a new user u is based on the following equation:*

$$i_u^* \simeq \underset{i \in D_u^{pool}}{\operatorname{argmin}} \sum_{j \in D_u^{test}} \left| r_{uj} - \hat{r}_{uj} + 2\alpha(\hat{r}_{ui} - r_{ui}) \sum_{f=1}^{k} h_{if} h_{jf} \right| \tag{6.16}$$

Proof. As our objective is to minimize the MAE of the new user u and on the other hand, based on MF, the ratings are calculated by the inner product between user and item parameters, the MAE can be rewritten as follows:

$$MAE_u = \frac{1}{|D_u^{test}|} \sum_{j \in D_u^{test}} \left| \sum_{f=1}^{k} w_{uf}^* h_{jf}^* - \sum_{f=1}^{k} w_{uf} h_{jf} \right| \tag{6.17}$$

where w^* and h^* are assumed to be the optimal user and item parameters in the latent space that ideally show how the latent factors influence the rating behavior of users and items. [1] The inner product of w_u^* and h_i^* will give us the actual rating r_{ui}.

Equation 6.17 is the current test error before asking a new query. The goal of the active learning algorithm is to minimize it in the next step (after getting a new rating) as much as possible by querying the best item. As we already mentioned, for retraining we exploit the online updating technique (Rendle & Schmidt-Thieme, 2008). Therefore, only the user parameters w_u change in the next step and item parameters h_i are fixed. Assuming that $l \geq 0$ items have been selected so far for user u, let w_{uf}^l denote the new user parameters (i.e. after the selection of l items) and define the test error in step l as :

$$MAE_u{}^l = \frac{1}{|D_u^{test}|} \sum_{j \in D_u^{test}} \left| \sum_{f=1}^{k} w_{uf}^* h_{jf}^* - \sum_{f=1}^{k} w_{uf}^l h_{jf} \right| \tag{6.18}$$

Therefore, it follows that the optimal query i^* is the one that produces the minimum $MAE_u{}^{l+1}$ by providing new user parameters w_{uf}^{l+1}:

$$i_u^* = \underset{i \in D_u^{pool}}{\operatorname{argmin}} \frac{1}{|D_u^{test}|} \sum_{j \in D_u^{test}} \left| \sum_{f=1}^{k} w_{uf}^* h_{jf}^* - \sum_{f=1}^{k} w_{uf}^{l+1} h_{jf} \right|. \tag{6.19}$$

Since $|D_u^{test}|$ is a constant number, it can be dropped from the previous equation, giving the following:

$$i_u^* = \underset{i \in D_u^{pool}}{\operatorname{argmin}} \sum_{j \in D_u^{test}} \left| \sum_{f=1}^{k} w_{uf}^* h_{jf}^* - \sum_{f=1}^{k} w_{uf}^{l+1} h_{jf} \right| \tag{6.20}$$

According to the law of the consistent estimator in statistics (Newey & Mcfadden, 1994), item parameters converge asymptotically to the true parameters, when there is infinity training data points. Typically, however, the convergence to the true parameters is reached earlier, since the difference – for large enough training sample sizes – between current and true item parameters is negligible. As the item parameters have been trained with training data including adequate number of ratings for each item, the

[1] As it is not possible to obtain w^* and h^* , we will later provide a simple and effective way to estimate them.

current item parameters approximate the true parameters well. Therefore, we can substitute h^*_{if} with h_{if}. Followed by a simple algebraic manipulation we will have:

$$i^*_u \simeq \operatorname*{argmin}_{i \in D^{pool}_u} \sum_{j \in D^{test}_u} \left| \sum_{f=1}^{k} (w^*_{uf} - w^{l+1}_{uf}) h_{jf} \right| \tag{6.21}$$

According to Equation 6.21, the optimal item to be selected is the one that will cause the updated user parameters w^{l+1}_{uf}, i.e. after the selected item (l + 1-th) is queried, to be as close as possible to the true user parameter w^*_{uf}. This is exactly what we already expected. The test error reduces as the accuracy of the estimation of the true user parameters improves.
Based on the Equation 6.4, we can express Equation 6.21 as follows:

$$i^*_u \simeq \operatorname*{argmin}_{i \in D^{pool}_u} \left(\sum_{j \in D^{test}_u} \left| \sum_{f=1}^{k} \Big(w^*_{uf} - w^l_{uf} + 2\alpha(\hat{r}_{ui} - r_{ui}) h_{if} \Big) h_{jf} \right| \right) \tag{6.22}$$

and with simple algebraic manipulations as follows:

$$i^*_u \simeq \operatorname*{argmin}_{i \in D^{pool}_u} \left(\sum_{j \in D^{test}_u} \left| \sum_{f=1}^{k} (w^*_{uf} - w^l_{uf}) h_{jf} + 2\alpha(\hat{r}_{ui} - r_{ui}) h_{if} h_{jf} \right| \right) \tag{6.23}$$

The inner product between w^l_u and h_j is equal to the predicted (by MF) rating, r_{uj} of user u for the test item j. Moreover, the inner product between w^*_u (the true user parameters of u) and the item parameters h_j for test item j correspond to the true rating. Based on the above, we have the following equation as a result:

$$i^*_u \simeq \operatorname*{argmin}_{i \in D^{pool}_u} \sum_{j \in D^{test}_u} \left| r_{uj} - \hat{r}_{uj} + 2\alpha(\hat{r}_{ui} - r_{ui}) \sum_{f=1}^{k} h_{if} h_{jf} \right| \tag{6.24}$$

□

It is worth comparing Equation 6.24 with Equation 2.2. The only difference in Equation 6.24 is the additional term $2\alpha(\hat{r}_{ui} - r_{ui}) \sum_{f=1}^{k} h_{if} h_{jf}$. This term actually predicts how retraining the new user parameters with the item i can remove the test error of the item j, which is $r_{uj} - \hat{r}_{uj}$. This is exactly what we are looking for. The aim of the proposed active learning is to decrease the test error, which is the summation of all errors of the test items. Therefore, it is reasonable to reach this term in the final equation. Another interesting point in Equation 6.24 is that the difference between the predicted rating $\hat{r}_{ui}$ and the true rating r_{ui} is weighted according to the inner product between h_i and h_j. This means that if the pool item i is close to the all test items j (i.e., small value of their inner product), then it is considered as more representative.

Equation 6.24 requires the knowledge of the actual rating r_{uj} to compute the test error $r_{uj} - \hat{r}_{uj}$. However, it is not possible to obtain r_{uj} since the rating of test data is unknown. To solve this problem, the proposed active learning method optimizes the query selection based on the worst test error. It means that given the test error of item j is the maximum, which item is the best item for query. The test error of item j is the maximum if the actual rating r_{uj} is different from what it is expected to be. In the datasets like MovieLens and Netflix, most of the ratings are higher than 3 (in Movielens 3.8 and in Netflix 3.6). Therefore, in order to find the upper-bound for test error, we substitute r_{uj} with 1. This approximation hopefully gives the worst test error and allows us to develop a robust active learning method. In this way, we are cautious and conservative about the current predicted ratings $\hat{r}_{uj}$ and rely on the active learning method on the upper-bound test error. Given that the learned model of the new user is not accurate (that is why we need to ask additional ratings), this simplification is reasonable and realistic.

Moreover, Equation 6.24 also requires the knowledge of actual pool item r_{uj}. However, it is not possible to obtain r_{ui} because the user u has to be first asked before providing a rating for them. Following a simple but effective approach, r_{ui} can be approximated by $\bar{R}_i$, which denotes the average rating of all training users for the item i. This simplification leads to the following criterion for item selection:

$$i_u^* \simeq \underset{i \in D_u^{pool}}{\operatorname{argmin}} \sum_{j \in D_u^{test}} \left| 1 - \hat{r}_{uj} + 2\alpha(\hat{r}_{ui} - \bar{R}_i) \sum_{f=1}^{k} h_{if} h_{jf} \right| \tag{6.25}$$

Based on Proposition 1, the criterion of Equation 6.25 is, therefore, aimed toward an optimal item selection. Evidently, the effectiveness of the applied approximation depends on the quality of the approximations of r_{ui} and r_{uj}. Our experimental results in the following section will indicate the effectiveness of the criterion proposed above. Nevertheless, we address the issue of investigating additional approximations for r_{uj} and r_{ui} as our main topic of future work.

6.5 Active Learning for Partial Oracle

So far, we have assumed that new users are able to rate all queried items. This assumption is necessary from the active learning point of view because in active learning the same assumption holds for the Oracle. However, in recommender systems this assumption is not realistic. Users may not have experienced the queried item, so they are unable to give ratings on them. For example, a user who has not watched a movie, cannot rate it. In this section, we develop active learning for the realistic scenario, in which new users are allowed not to rate the queried items. We still stick with online updating to retrain the new user parameters after getting new ratings. In fact, this is preliminary work and in the next two chapters, we will address this scenario more deeply using approaches other than online updating.

There is a trade-off between the information-theoretic value of a new rating and the likelihood of a user being able to provide a rating. A comprehensive method should take both criteria into account. However, in this section we take into account only the likelihood factor and address the comprehensive solution in the next two chapters. Therefore, we aim to choose a query that is likely to be answered by the new user.

As the process of active learning starts without any rating from the new user and ends up just with a few queries (e.g. 10 queries), relying solely on the new user's answers does not provide *enough* information to find suitable queries specially when the number of items is large. An appropriate solution to address this problem is to link the new user to the training users and exploit available information from them. We use the characteristics of matrix factorization, as the predictive model of the recommender system, to make such a connection.

When the training of the matrix factorization is done, users and items are mapped into the latent space. Users (or items) with similar rating behaviors are mapped into the same region. We exploit this characteristic of matrix factorization to find users who are similar to the new user. Then the item that is most popular *among the similar users* is selected for the next query. Hopefully, the new user is able to provide a rating for an item that has already been rated by users with similar rating behavior. In this way, the drawback of the global most popular, which asks *static* queries regardless of the answers of the new user, is fixed while the new user is connected to the training users to exploit their information. The number of similar users s is a hyper parameter. It should not be too large because it affects the scalability.

Algorithm 8 describes the proposed method, which we call Most Popular in Latent Space (MPLS). First, we train an MF model with the training dataset including all training users. Then, we start asking new users queries. In the beginning, when the new user has not given any rating, all training users are considered as similar users. Therefore, the first queried item is the most popular item. According to the new user's answer to the first query, a subset of the training users who have the same answer to the first queried item are selected as the similar users and the second query, is the most popular item among them. In any step, if the new user provides a rating to the queried item, the new user parameters are retrained using online updating. The interview continues until N queries.

The accuracy of the proposed method depends heavily on how good the similar users found are. If the similar users are correct, then approximating the rating behavior of the new user using the similar users is also accurate. Otherwise, performance will be affected. In order to find similar users, we use cosine similarity because in matrix factorization the ratings are predicted by the inner product of user and item parameters, so it makes sense to stick with the same similarity measure for active-learning purposes as well.

Algorithm 8 The Algorithm of Most Popular in Latent Space (MPLS)

Input: $\mathcal{D}^{\text{train}}$, N, s
Output: $\mathcal{D}_u^{query}$

Train MF with $\mathcal{D}^{train}$
loop {repeats until N queries}
  Find s similar users to the target user
  Find the most popular item among the similar users
  Ask the new user to rate item i^*
  if user provides a rating **then**
    $\mathcal{D}_u^{query} = \mathcal{D}_u^{query} \cup (i^*, r)$
    Update new user parameters with $\mathcal{D}_u^{query}$
  end if
end loop

6.6 Experimental Result

In this section, we experimentally examine the performance of the proposed methods. This section consists of two parts. In the first part, we compare active learning methods for the full Oracle, i.e. methods that assume the new user always rates the queried items. Next, we report the results of active learning for the partial Oracle, meaning new users are allowed not to rate the queries. We use MovieLens dataset to evaluate active learning methods for full Oracle. The details of the evaluation protocol and how the data set is split were already explained in chapter 2.

6.6.1 Results for Full Oracle

In this chapter, we have defined four active learning criteria for full Oracle. We start evaluations with non-myopic active learning and then we compare all methods with one another. The reason for evaluating the non-myopic method separately is that it consists of two algorithms (exploration and exploitation) and it is necessary to study those algorithms as well to understand the behavior of this approach. In the other hand, drawing many curves in a single chart makes it difficult to understand how they are performing.

Non-myopic active learning consists of two algorithms: the smallest predicted rating (MinRating) for exploration , the smallest item parameters norm (MinNorm) for exploitation. Also, we defined MaxNorm (largest item parameters norm) as an alternative for MinRating. So in total we need to compare four algorithms plus the random baseline. Figure 6.4 illustrates the comparison between these four methods in terms of MAE as a function of the number of queried items.

Clearly, the non-myopic method compares favorably to the other methods. This happens because it takes the advantage of both exploration and exploitation algorithms. In the first queries that exploration is necessary, MinRating competes with non-myopic.

However, the MinRating's performance does not continue because it never exploits. To clearly understand the role of exploration and exploitation, we need to look at the gradient. Table 6.1 depicts the gradient after each queried item for all methods (total of 10 queried items). The gradient of the MinRating is larger than the other methods in almost all the queries. This is useful at the beginning because it leads to exploration. But it does not help as more ratings are provided by the new user. Another interesting result in table 6.1 is about the MinNorm. The gradient of the MinNorm is smaller than the other methods and so, its accuracy is much worse than random. This shows that exploitation alone does not work and it should be combined with the exploration algorithm. Finally, the gradient of the MinRating is larger than the MaxNorm. It shows that, as we expected, to maximize the the gradient, we need to focus more on the prediction error than item parameters. This leads to better accuracy, especially in the first queries.

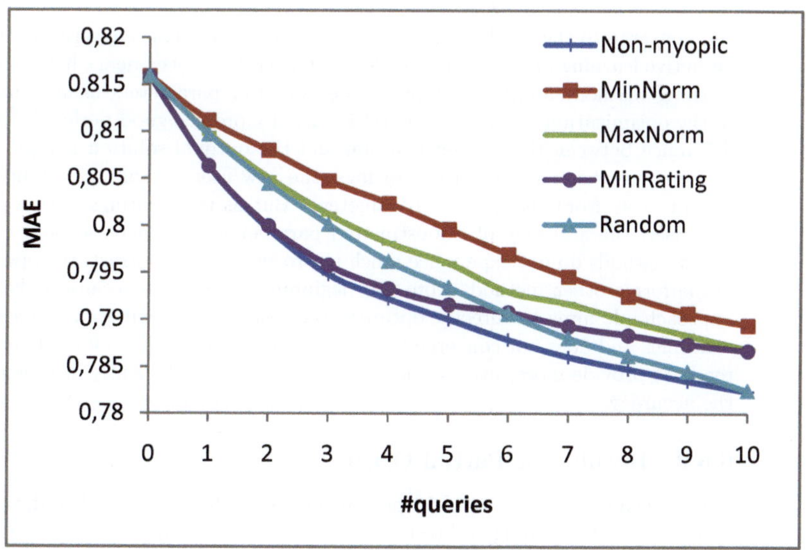

Figure 6.4: MAE results of the MinRating (exploration), MinNorm (exploitation), Non-myopic (combination of exploration and exploitation), MaxNorm (items with large parameters norm) , and random

Now we go on to compare all four proposed criteria in this chapter. Figure 6.5 shows the results of optimal, non-myopic uncertainty in the rating space (RatingUnc) and uncertainty in the latent space (LatentUnc). Non-myopic, RatingUnc and LatentUnc exhibit more or less the same behavior. They perform well in the first queries but at the

Table 6.1: The gradient after each query for all proposed criteria

# query	Non-myopic	MinRating	MinNorm	MaxNorm	Random
1	-0.165	-0.177	-0.060	-0.061	-0.065
2	-0.177	-0.207	-0.063	-0.073	-0.083
3	-0.184	-0.173	-0.022	-0.069	-0.051
4	-0.160	-0.163	-0.013	-0.084	-0.083
5	-0.120	-0.151	-0.047	-0.028	-0.023
6	-0.122	-0.177	-0.029	-0.023	-0.060
7	-0.117	-0.098	-0.001	-0.046	-0.058
8	-0.037	-0.092	-0.018	-0.051	-0.021
9	-0.054	-0.068	0.026	0.042	-0.024
10	0.050	-0.098	-0.013	-0.027	-0.046

end converge to the random selection (see Figure 6.4). This convergence also happens for active learning in AM (Jin & Si, 2004). Generally, this evidence holds true for active learning methods aiming to improve the new user parameters using some heuristics. In the optimization theory, the heuristics usually provide good performance only if the difference between the current solution and the optimal solution is high. At first, as the new user has provided a few ratings, the new user parameters are inaccurate and are far away from the optimal parameters. But as more ratings are provided by the new user, the accuracy of the estimated parameters also increases and the heuristic-based methods do not experience much improvement. In contrast, the optimal method outperforms other methods from the beginning to the end because it has a different approach. It aims to directly optimize the test error. That is why its performance continues and does not converge to the random selection. Therefore, if the new user is ready to provide more ratings, the optimal method can efficiently use them to improve the accuracy.

6.6.2 Results for Partial Oracle

For this experiment, we used 50 percent of the Netflix dataset. The dataset was randomly split into training and test sets, containing 70% and 30% respectively. Each test user was considered as a new user. 30% of the ratings of each test user were separated to compute the error (test data) and the queries were selected from the remaining items (pool data). In our experiment, 10 queries were asked to each new user.

Figure 6.6 illustrates the comparison between MPLS, non-myopic active learning, and most popular selection in terms of RMSE as a function of the number of queried items.

In the first queries, the most popular method competes with the MPLS. This happens because during the first queries, little knowledge has been revealed about the rating behavior of the new user. Therefore, it is difficult to find *real* similar users. But

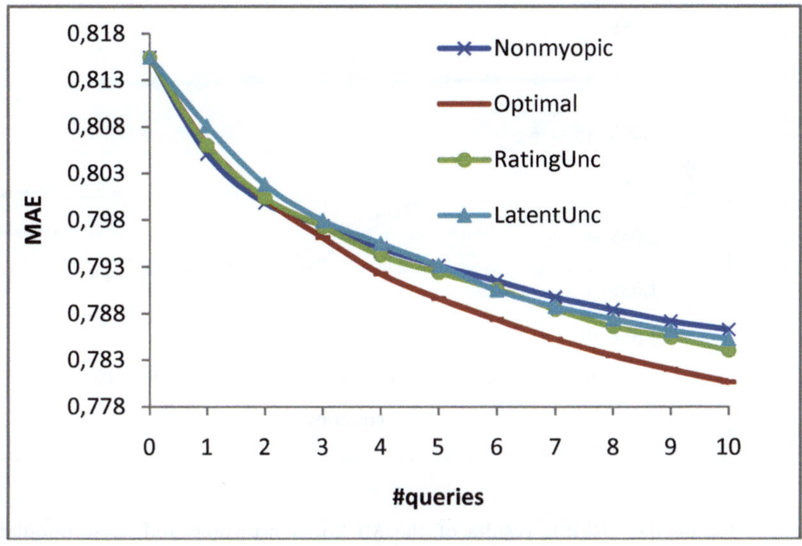

Figure 6.5: MAE results of Optimal, Non-myopic, Uncertainty in the rating space (RatingUnc), and uncertainty in the latent space (LatentUnc)

as more ratings are provided by the new user, the similar users become closer to the real similar users, which consequently increases the probability that the new user will provide an answer to the queried item. Another interesting observation in Figure 6.6 is that the non-myopic method does not work at all. This was expected to happen because this method only aims to choose a query that reduces the test error and supposes that the new user is always able to provide a rating to the queried item. However, we have relaxed this assumption, meaning that the queried item may not get a rating. Obviously, this assumption has a significant effect on the performance of active learning methods.

The performance of the active learning methods depends on the number of ratings provided by the new user. The more the ratings, the better the performance. Table 6.2 shows the average number of ratings provided by a new user after ten queries. The proposed method receives more ratings compared to most popular while the non-myopic method receives almost no ratings.

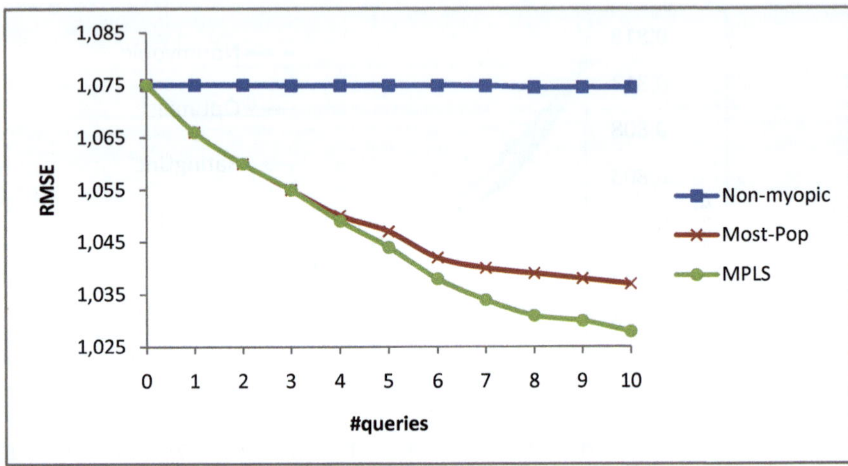

Figure 6.6: RMSE results of the MPLS, non-myopic and most popular versus the number of queries

Table 6.2: The average number of ratings received from the new user after 10 queries

Method	#Ratings
MPLS	2.6468
Most Pop	2.6374
Non-myopic	0.0007

6.7 Summary and Future Work

In this chapter, after being inspired by the literature of active learning for machine learning, we introduced four active learning criteria for MF. Two methods are based on uncertainty. The first uncertainty criterion (LatentUnc) is based on the characteristics of MF and opts for selecting the items that are most sensitive to the inaccurate estimation of user parameters. The second uncertainty measure (RatingUnc) computes the difference between the current prediction of items by the recommendation model and the predictions given by the item average.

Following the non-myopic active learning approach in machine learning, we developed a non-myopic active learning method for MF. It is based on the exploration/

exploitation dilemma. First, it explores the latent space to get closer to the optimal new user parameters. Then, it exploits the learned parameters and adjusts them slightly.

We applied the principle of optimal active learning (Cohn *et al.*, 1995) in MF and with some approximations, we derived a closed-form criterion that approximates the optimal solution for recommender systems. The optimal active learning selects a query that directly optimizes the expected error in the test data. This approach is applicable for prediction models in which this question can be answered in closed form. Nevertheless, we could exploit the characteristics of matrix factorization and derive a closed-form solution.

Finally, we relaxed the assumption of full Oracle for new users and developed an active learning for partial Oracle. The partial Oracle means users may not rate the queried items. Our method (MPLS) improves the most popular selection strategy using the characteristics of matrix factorization. It finds similar users to the new user in the latent space and then selects the item that is most popular *among the similar users*. The results showed that MPLS received more ratings from new users compared to the most popular selection.

As the future work, we can think about applying other active learning techniques of machine learning to recommender systems. For example, in chapter 3, we mentioned some active learning methods that cluster the pool data and select the representative of clusters. The goal is to obtain training data that covers the whole of the data space. One could apply this approach in MF. It means clustering the items in the latent space and selecting the items that are representative of clusters. As items with different behavior in receiving ratings from users are mapped into different regions of the latent space, clustering can efficiently distinguish them and provide a set of items that represent whole items of the dataset. Another possibility is to cluster users in the latent space and then try to find the right cluster of the new user by posing queries that effectively identify the right cluster. At the end, the new user parameters can be retrained with all ratings of the users of the target cluster.

In this chapter, we used standard MF. There are other kinds of MF that might be more suitable for active learning, e.g. probabilistic MF. As this model provides a probabilistic interpretation, it could be more straightforward and convenient to define uncertainty for active learning.

To drive optimal active learning, we relied on some simplifications to replace the actual ratings of test items and pool items. Although the results showed the simplifications were effective, we can still think about better solutions for this regard, for example, global average or the user average of similar users.

Finally, we can change the setting of the problem in a way that the new users are queried for more than one item during each interaction with recommender systems. A page showing a couple of items is shown to new users and they may rate one or more items on the page. In this case, we should study batch-mode active learning techniques and then adapt them for new user problems in recommender systems. Batch-mode active learning is more challenging because, in addition to selecting informative queries, diversity should also be taken into account. This means that items in a single batch should not have similar attributes, because they provide the same information to the system.

Chapter 7

Factorized Decision Trees

(Golbandi *et al.*, 2011) was a breakthrough in the literature on active learning for recommender systems. Therefore, we decided to switch to this framework for the rest of my thesis and find ways on how to improve it. Four ideas, which will be presented in this chapter, extend (Golbandi *et al.*, 2011) and provide a new framework for active learning in recommender systems (Karimi *et al.*, 2013). Like (Golbandi *et al.*, 2011), we let users not rate queried items, meaning we consider new users as partial Oracle.

7.1 Problem Formulation

In chapter 2, we formalized the problem of active learning for recommender systems, given that new users are full Oracle, meaning they are able to rate all queried items. As in this chapter, we are going to relax the constrain of full Oracle for new users, we provide a new formulation that is slightly different from the formulation of chapter 2. Also, in this formulation it is supposed that active learning methods use multivariate (vector-value target) regression trees.

Let U be a set (of users), I be another set (of items), and $R \subseteq \mathbb{R}$ be a (finite) set of ratings, e.g., $R := \{1, 2, 3, 4, 5\}$. Let $R^+ := R \cup \{.\}$ with an additional symbol for a missing value. Denote by a triple $(u, i, r) \in U \times I \times R$ a rating r of user u for item i.

For a data set $D \subseteq U \times I \times R$ denote the set of all users occurring in D by

$$U(D) := \{u \in U \mid (u, i, r) \in D\}$$

Subsets $E \subseteq I \times R$ are called user profiles. The profile of user u in D is denoted by

$$D_u := \{(i, r) \in I \times R \mid (u, i, r) \in D\}$$

The rating of item $i \in I$ in user profile $E \subseteq I \times R$ is denoted by

$$r(i; E) := \begin{cases} r & , \text{if } (i, r) \in E \\ . & , \text{else} \end{cases}$$

A tree where each interior node is labeled with an item $i \in I$, each branch with a rating value $r \in R^+$ and each leaf node with a rating predictive model $\hat{r} : I \to R$ is called a questionnaire. For a user profile $E \subseteq I \times R$ let $\hat{R}(E)$ denote the rating predictive model at the leaf one arrives when starting at the root of the tree and iteratively from a node with label $i \in I$ proceeds to its child node with label $r(i; E)$ until a leaf node is reached.

Given

- a data set $\mathcal{D}^{\text{train}} \subseteq U \times I \times R$,
- a loss $\ell : R \times \mathbb{R} \to \mathbb{R}$, and
- a maximal number of queries N,

the active learning for recommender systems problems is to find a questionnaire $\hat{R}$ of maximal depth N s.t. for another data set $\mathcal{D}^{\text{test}} \subseteq U \times I \times R$ (sampled from the same distribution, not being used during training, and with non-overlapping users, i.e., $U(\mathcal{D}^{\text{train}}) \cap U(\mathcal{D}^{\text{test}}) = \emptyset$) the average loss is minimal.

Users in $\mathcal{D}^{\text{test}}$ are supposed to be new users. For each $u \in \mathcal{D}^{\text{test}}$, $\mathcal{D}_u$ is split into $\mathcal{D}_u^{\text{pool}}$ (pool data) and $\mathcal{D}_u^{\text{test}}$ (test data). $\mathcal{D}_u^{\text{pool}}$ is used to find the predictive model $\hat{R}(\mathcal{D}_u^{\text{pool}})$ at the leaf node and $\mathcal{D}_u^{\text{test}}$ is used to evaluate it. $\mathcal{D}_u^{\text{pool}}$ should also contain items with missing value, so

$$\mathcal{D}_u^{\text{pool}} = \mathcal{D}_u^{\text{pool}} \cup \{(u, i, .) | i \in I, i \notin \mathcal{D}_u^{\text{pool}}\}$$

The total loss is the loss over all test users:

$$\ell(\mathcal{D}^{\text{test}}; \hat{R}) := \frac{1}{|\mathcal{D}^{\text{test}}|} \sum_{u \in U(\mathcal{D}^{\text{test}})} \sum_{(i,y) \in \mathcal{D}_u^{\text{test}}} \ell(y, \hat{R}(\mathcal{D}_u^{\text{pool}})(i)) \tag{7.1}$$

7.2 Active Learning or Bootstrapping?

The cold-start problem in recommender systems is usually studied from the perspective of active learning because of an analogy between this problem and a similar problem that exists in the machine learning community. In supervised machine learning, there is sometimes not enough labeled data to train a model. But there is a set of unlabeled data and it is possible to request the labels from an oracle. However, querying the labels is costly. Therefore, a few instances from the unlabeled data set are selected for querying but only those that are effective in improving the accuracy of the model. This situation is very similar to the new user problem in recommender system. As the new user has not rated any item, it is not possible to train a personalized model for the new user. But there are many items and we can ask the new user to rate (label) them. However, the new user does not wish to be queried too many times. Therefore, a few items should be selected for querying but only those that are effective in improving the new user model. Due to this analogy, techniques that are used to ask new users to rate items are usually called *active learning for recommender systems* (Harpale & Yang, 2008; Jin & Si, 2004; Karimi *et al.*, 2011b,c, 2012a).

However, (Golbandi *et al.*, 2011) do not explicitly call their works active learning and prefer to name their method *Bootstrapping.* Although the names are different, they have the same basic goal: to learn new user preferences as much as possible with a few questions. In order to make this more clear, we need to compare Equation 7.1 with Equation 4.13.

As one can find out, in Bootstrapping the best item is the item that minimizes the *training error* (Equation 4.13). But in active learning, the best item is the item that minimizes the *test error* (Equation 7.1). Despite this difference, Bootstrapping is not inconsistent with active learning methods after all. We can consider the Bootstrapping approach as a solution to replace the test data, which is not available in the training phase, especially as there is already a paper in the literature on active learning that has more or less a similar approach. (Nicholas & McCallum, 2001) replaces $\mathcal{D}^{\text{test}}$ with $\mathcal{D}^{\text{pool}}$ to estimate how candidate examples would reduce the test error.

7.3 Decision Tree or Decision Process?

The way that decision trees are used in (Golbandi *et al.*, 2011) poses some ambiguities. In this section, we would like to clarify this ambiguity.

In machine learning, decision trees are predictive models in which leaves represent the values of target variable and branches represent conjunctions of input features that lead to those values. There are two types of decision trees: classification trees and regression trees. Classification trees are used when the the target variable is a nominal variable and in the case of a numerical target variable, regression trees are used.

Coming back to the new user problem in recommender systems, we can look at this problem from two different perspectives. In the first view, we define this problem as a decision-making problem. Namely, there is a user and we want to decide which item must be selected to ask its rating from that user. So, decisions are items. To learn the correct decisions, we use training data and measure the outcome of each decision and finally pick the best item. Obviously, this is *not* a decision tree that is used in machine learning because there is no target variable in the leaf nodes. In fact, it is a decision process that is used in data analysis to visually and explicitly represent decisions. In data mining, a decision tree describes data but not decisions and the resulting decision tree can be an input for decision making.

Now let's look at the new user problem from a different perspective. There is a new user who has not given any ratings. Therefore, recommender systems are not able to predict ratings for that new user because they are based on collaborative filtering and in collaborative filtering we need to compare the ratings of users to find similar users and then take the average over similar users. As the new user has not provided any rating, it is not possible to find similar users. To solve this problem, we want to ask the new user to give a rating to an item. Then, using this rating, we find similar users, i.e. users who have given the same rating to the queried item, and using the ratings of the similar users, we predict the rating for the new user, like a typical collaborative filtering. Now the question is which item is the best item to query from the new user. We can learn such items using the training data (the details can be found in section 4.2.3). Depending on the new user's rating to the queried item, similar users are different. Decision trees can be used to graphically and visually represent this situation. In this tree, each possible answer is shown as a branch and similar users are placed in the corresponding child node. Constructing decision trees continues to a specific depth that corresponds to the number of queries. In the leaves of decision trees, the ratings of similar users are used for rating predictions for new users who will end up there. Now we have a *regression tree*. In this regression tree, the target variables are predicted ratings for items. As there is more than one item, the target variable is a multivariate variable. Therefore, we can call this tree a *multivariate (vector-value target) regression tree* (Larsen & Speckman, 2004; Segal, 1992; Zhang, 1998) with values in $\mathbb{R}^I$. In the rest of this thesis, we consider decision trees as multivariate regression trees that are used to find items for query that result in the minimum error in rating predictions for new users. Note that in some works, a multivariate tree refers to a tree in which nodes are split based on more than one input feature, which is not what we mean in this thesis.

In the end, it is worth mentioning that there is a small amount of literature on *model tree* (Landwehr *et al.*, 2005; Rodríguez *et al.*, 2010). Model trees are decision trees that have models at their leaves to provide predictions. In contrast to decision trees, which have constants at the leaves, in model trees the predictions at the leaves are different, depending on the attributes of the instances. This means that if two instances end up on the same leaf but they have different attributes, they may also have different predictions. We cannot consider (Golbandi *et al.*, 2011) as model trees because in (Golbandi *et al.*, 2011) the item predictions at a given leaf are the same for all users who belong to that leaf node.

7.4 Factorized Decision Trees

In (Golbandi *et al.*, 2011), the ratings are predicted based on the item average, which may seem naive as there are more advanced algorithms, such as MF, which have already shown their superiority over the item average. The reason for using the item average is that building decision trees is expensive in terms of time. There are many nodes that need to be expanded and per each node there are many candidate items which must be checked. As a result, we need a method for rating prediction that is fast, even though it may not be the best method. Otherwise, building decision trees would be intractable.

Now the question is "how can we improve rating prediction of decision trees while keeping its complexity low?" To find a solution for this question, we divide the learning algorithm of decision trees into two steps. In the first step, the *structure* of decision trees is learned. Then, we learn the *labels* of the tree where the labels are the ratings. The structure is learned exactly according to (Golbandi *et al.*, 2011). And to learn the labels, MF is used. We call our method "Factorized Decision Trees (FDT)".

To incorporate MF into the decision trees, we should take into account how users have been partitioned in the tree. Initially, all users are at the root. Then they are partitioned into three groups based on their answer to the first selected query. Each child node represents a set of users who have the same answer to the queried item. As each user goes to one of the child nodes at level 1, the union of the associated users of all nodes gives us a complete set of users. This phenomena is true for all levels and training users have been completely partitioned among the leaves of the tree. Therefore, we consider one MF model for the last level of decision trees.

Formally, let $V_l := \{t_1, ..., t_n\}$ be a set of nodes at level l. We define a set of pseudo users $U_l = \{u_1, ..., u_n\}$, in which u_i represents node t_i. The ratings of each pseudo user u_i is the union of all the ratings users associated with the corresponding node t_i. An MF model is trained with $|U_l|$ users and $|I|$ items. In this way, MF is trained using the complete version of the dataset while the structure of the tree is also retained. Figures 7.1 and 7.2 show how FDT works for one and two queries.

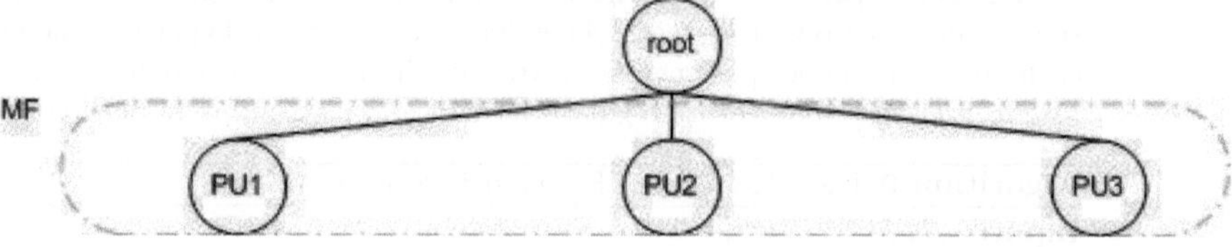

Figure 7.1: A decision tree with depth 1. MF is trained for level 1 with three pseudo users.

Algorithm 9 describes the details of FDT. At first, the *structure* of the decision trees is learned according to (Golbandi *et al.*, 2011) with a minor difference. (Golbandi *et al.*, 2011) randomize the item selection process in the way that items that more significantly reduce the error would have more chances to be selected as splitters. Randomization is useful for online evaluations and also for asking new users to rate multiple items in each query. As we do not conduct online evaluation and also ask new users to provide rating only for one item in each query, randomization is removed and the splitter item is selected in a fully deterministic manner.

After constructing the tree, post-processing is done on top of the tree to learn the *labels* of the tree, i.e. the rating predictions. For each level, the best hyper-parameters of MF are found and then MF is retrained with those parameters. Finally, the predictions are updated using MF. We do not exploit MF during tree construction because it causes too much complexity. We will discuss that later. At level 0, the root of the tree, there

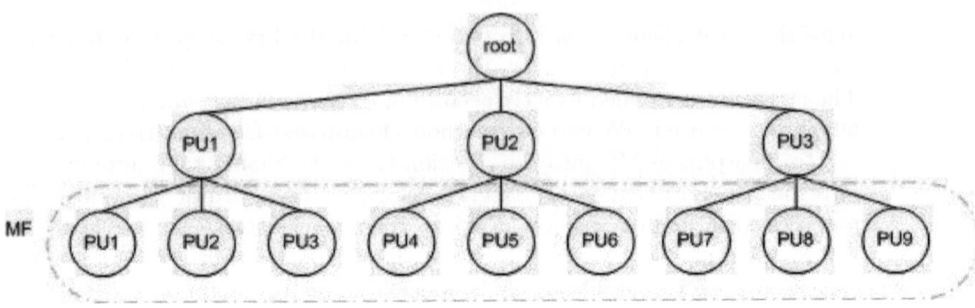

Figure 7.2: A decision tree with depth 2. MF is trained for level 2 with nine pseudo users.

is only one node. This means we should train an MF with one pseudo user, which does not make sense. Therefore, for the root node we switch to the item average method for rating prediction as it is done in (Golbandi *et al.*, 2011).

The maximum level of the tree is N, which is the maximum number of queries. As the number of pseudo users varies in trees with different depths, the data set of each tree is different from other trees. Therefore, we have to do hyper-parameter search for each tree. The hyper-parameters of MF are the number of latent factors k, learning rate α, user and item feature regularization λ, and user and item bias regularization γ.

Algorithm 9 The Algorithm of Factorized Decision Trees

Input: N, $\mathcal{D}^{\text{train}}$, $\mathcal{D}^{val}$,
Output: W, H, $\hat{R}$

Construct decision trees with $\mathcal{D}^{\text{train}}$ according to (Golbandi *et al.*, 2011) up to level N
$\alpha^*, \lambda^* \leftarrow 0, min\_err = +\infty$
for each α in 0.0001 to 0.01 **do**
  for each λ in 0.001 to 0.03 **do**
    Train MF for the level N
    Compute error on the validation data $\mathcal{D}^{val}$
    if error $< min\_err$ **then**
      $\alpha^* \leftarrow \alpha, \lambda^* \leftarrow \lambda, min\_err = error$
    end if
  end for
end for
Retrain MF with the best hyper-parameters (α^*, λ^*)
Update rating predictions of pseudo users at level N

7.4.1 Complexity Analysis of FDT

In order to analyze the complexity of FDT, first we need to know the complexity of Bootstrapping (Golbandi *et al.*, 2011) because FDT relies on it to build the tree. The complexity of Bootstrapping is $O(N \cdot |\mathcal{D}|^2)$ (Golbandi *et al.*, 2011). According to the algorithm 9, FDT would also have the same complexity, plus the overhead of training the MF model at each level of the decision trees. On the other hand, the time complexity of MF is $O(|\mathcal{D}| \cdot k \cdot L)$ (Rendle & Schmidt-Thieme, 2008). Hence, the total time complexity of FDT is $O(N \cdot |\mathcal{D}|^2 + |\mathcal{D}| \cdot k \cdot L)$. Compared to the time complexity of functional matrix factorization (fmf) (Zhou *et al.*, 2011), FDT is much less complicated. As it was pointed out in section 4.2, the complexity of fmf is $O(N \sum_{u \in U} |\mathcal{D}_u|^2 + l|I|k^3 + l|I|^2k^2)$, which makes it really slow for large datasets like Netflix.

So far, MF did not play any role in building the tree. The tree is built according to (Golbandi *et al.*, 2011) and afterwards MF is used to change the predicted ratings at each node. But this is not optimal. Now that MF is used for rating prediction, the best split item of each node is the one which reduces the error of MF, not the average. However, choosing the split item of each node based on MF poses challenges, which makes it intractable.

Suppose we want to select the q-th query. This means that we are in a node at the $(q-1)$-th level of decision trees. For this node, there are $|I| - q - 1$ candidate items. The best item is the one that minimizes the error of MF in the next level. However, to train MF, we need to expand all the nodes at level $q-1$ to generate a new dataset including all pseudo users at level q. Therefore, the best item selected of each node is not independent of the rest of the nodes that exist at the same level. This means we have to check all selections and choose the one with the minimum error. However, checking all selections would be very expensive. At level l, there are 3^l nodes, therefore the total number of selections that must be examined is $(|I| - i - 1)^{3^l}$. On the other hand, the time complexity of the matrix factorization learning algorithm is $O(L \times |\mathcal{D}| \times k)$ (Rendle & Schmidt-Thieme, 2008). Therefore, the complexity of finding the best q-th query is $O((|I| - i - 1)^{3^{q-1}} \times L \times |\mathcal{D}| \times k)$. Obviously, constructing the tree in this way would be intractable.

7.4.2 Null and Deadlock Nodes

In general, the number of nodes at level i is 3^i and the number of users is equal in all levels. However, there are two situations where this general rule is broken. Suppose we are at level i. While we are splitting nodes, we might encounter a node where, among its associated users, there is no user who has a specific answer to the split item. For example, there is no user who likes the split item. In that case, the node of the missing answer is created but it is null, i.e. it has no associated users. When nodes at level $i+1$ are split, the null node is not split because it has no associated user. Thus, the number of nodes at level $i+2$ would be $3^{(i+2)} - 3$ because the three child nodes of the null node are missing in level $i+2$.

The second situation happens when a node is split but the summation of errors at child nodes is larger than the error at the current node. According to (Golbandi *et al.*, 2011), such nodes are not expanded. This means again that the number of nodes at the next level would be three nodes less than the expected number. Moreover, as the associated users of such nodes get stuck in the current node, the number of users in the next level would also be lower than the number of users in the current level. We call these nodes *deadlock* nodes. In our experiments, from level 6 to 8, we observed a few null and deadlock nodes.

7.5 Further Improvements in FDT

In this section, we propose three methods to speed up FDT and make it more accurate.

7.5.1 Most Popular Sampling

In section 7.4, we proposed a method which makes the rating predictions of decision trees more accurate. In this section, we want to improve decision trees from a different point of view and make it faster.

A naive construction of the tree would be intractable if the number of items and ratings is large. Therefore, (Golbandi *et al.*, 2011) proposes a solution for that. The idea is to expand "Unknown" child nodes in a different way using some statistics collected from "Like" and "Dislike" child nodes. In this section, we propose a sampling method to make the tree construction algorithm even faster. This method is called Most Popular Sampling (MPS).

In each node, instead of checking all candidate items, only those which are popular among users associated with the node are examined. Formally, let $I' := \{i \in I \mid Rank(i) < M\}$ in which $Rank(i)$ is the popularity ranking of item i and M is the sampling size. Then the equation (4.13) is changed as follows:

$$splitter(t) = \underset{i \in I'}{\operatorname{argmin}} \; Err_t(i) \tag{7.2}$$

To understand why this heuristic works, one needs to return to a challenge that exists in recommender systems. In recommender systems, users usually provide few ratings. Therefore, many items do not receive ratings from most of the users. If the candidate item is not popular, most of the users go to the "Unknown" child node. In this case, the predictions in the "Unknown" child node would not be significantly different from the predictions in the current node because the associate users of two nodes and consequently the mean ratings are the same. Moreover, as the number of users in "Like" and "Dislike" nodes are not many, the predictions at these nodes are heavily regularized towards the predictions in the current node. Therefore, the predictions at these nodes do not significantly improve, either. However, splitting nodes with popular items distributes users more or less uniformly among child nodes. This would lead to new predictions that do not suffer from the mentioned problems.

7.5.2 6-way Split

(Golbandi *et al.*, 2011) opts for 3-way splits corresponding to three possible user responses ("like","dislike", and "unknown"). In a dataset with ratings in the range of 1 to 5, the ratings 1, 2, and 3 mean "dislike", and ratings 4 and 5 are considered as "like". Also, there is one child node for the case where the new user does not know the queried item ("unknown"). However, it is expected that a more refined split, such as a 6-way split that matches five star levels plus an "unknown" would improve accuracy. The main bottleneck to do so is the overhead caused by increasing the number of nodes. The higher the number of splits, the higher the number of nodes, which requires more time to build decision trees. To make this overhead more clear, we provide an example. Suppose that decision trees are built up to level 6. Given a 3-way split, the total number of nodes is $\sum_{l=0}^{6} 3^l = 1093$. But if the nodes are split based on the 6-way split, decision trees would have $\sum_{l=0}^{6} 6^l = 55987$ nodes. Clearly, increasing the number of splits exponentially grows the number of nodes.

Fortunately, we have already proposed MPS to speed up the tree construction algorithm. Therefore, given that MPS is used, a 6-way split can be used to improve the accuracy of rating predictions while the decision tree learning algorithm is still tractable.

7.5.3 Warm FDT

As it was already pointed out, FDT builds one MF model for the last level of the decision trees. The number of items is the same in all trees but the number of pseudo users varies according to the number of nodes in the last level. As there is a hierarchical relationship between the nodes of the decision trees, it would be useful to exploit this relationship when MF models are trained. A straightforward way to this end is to initialize the user features of each node by using the user features of its parent node. As users of child nodes have a rating behavior similar to their parent nodes, it makes sense to start the learning of user features from their parent features and then continue the learning to make them more precise. Therefore, the initialization is done as follows:

$$w_{uf} = w^p_{uf} + \mathcal{N}(0, 0.001)$$

where w_{uf} is the f-the feature of user u and w^p_{uf} is the corresponding feature of its parent node. We add a little noise for initialization. The noise has a Normal distribution with mean 0 and variance 0.001. In this way, we need to train two MF models for a tree: one for the N-th level and one for the level $N-1$. Furthermore, the item features can also be initialized with the item features that have already been learned in the previous level. Usually in the literature, this way of initialization is called online updating or warm restart (Bottou, 1998; Mairal *et al.*, 2010). Note that as there is no MF at level 0, i.e the root of the decision trees, the user features at level 1 are initialized randomly.

7.6 Experimental Result

In this section, we experimentally examine the performance of the proposed methods.

7.6.1 Experimental Setup

In our experiment, 8 or 10 queries are asked to each new user. We compare our methods to Bootstrapping (Golbandi *et al.*, 2011), which we implemented ourselves in java. First, we followed the same hyper-parameters reported in (Golbandi *et al.*, 2011) to calibrate our results against it and make sure that our implementation was correct. However, in our experiments we changed one of the hyper-parameters: (Golbandi *et al.*, 2011) does not expand nodes in which the the number of ratings is fewer than $\alpha = 200000$ and stops the learning. The goal is to save runtime. In our experiments, we set α to zero because MPS is already able to save runtime and there is no need to stop the learning. The results show that this setting is significantly beneficial. For $\alpha = 200000$, the RMSE is 0.971 after 5 queries but for $\alpha = 0$ the RMSE would be 0.958. Also, for $\alpha = 200000$ the learning converges after 6 queries, but for $\alpha = 0$ it continues until the 8th query.

To regenerate the reported results of this paper, the way that the parameters are initialized should be taken into account. The parameters of MF are initialized randomly with a normal distribution of $N(0, 001)$. A sequence of random numbers are generated to initialize user features, item features, user bias, item bias, and finally to shuffle the dataset and choose a random instance (u, i, r) for the stochastic gradient descent.

As (Golbandi *et al.*, 2011) conduct their experiment on the Netflix dataset, we also run our experiments on this dataset. In chapter 2, we mentioned how this dataset is split. Before reporting the results of our contributions, we would like to compare Bootstrapping to three baselines to show that the new user problem in recommender systems is a difficult problem and demands mature solutions. These three baselines are as follows:

- **Random:** At each node, the split item is selected randomly.
- **Local Most Popular (LMP):** At each node, the most popular item according to the users associated with the node is selected. It is equal to the MPS when the sampling size is 1.
- **Global Most Popular (GMP):** First, s most popular items are found based on all ratings available in the dataset. Then we start to build decision trees. All the

nodes that are at level l are expanded using the l-th most popular item. In this way, the dynamic aspect of decision trees is omitted and all new users, regardless of their responses to the queries, receive the same questions.

The results of the contributions will be presented in the same order as they have been introduced in this paper: we start with MPS. Then we report the results of FDT. The 6-way split is discussed in the third part and we conclude this section with the results of warm FDT.

7.6.2 Results

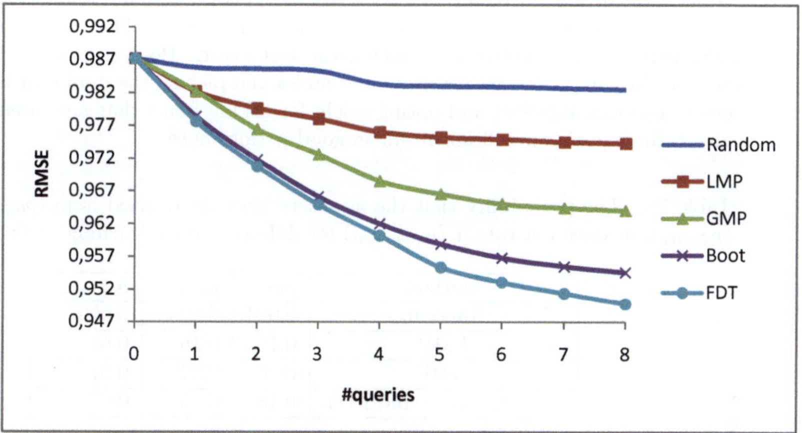

Figure 7.3: RMSE results of FDT, Bootstrapping and three baselines: Random, Local Most Popular (LMP), and Global Most Popular (GMP)

Figure 7.3 shows the results of three simple baselines, Bootstrapping and FDT. As the results show, random item selection performs very badly and gains almost nothing after 8 queries. LMP doesn't work well either. Among the three simple baselines, GMP is the best, although it is still much worse than Bootstrapping. Table 7.1 shows some statistics which can justify these results. This table shows the probabilities of receiving different responses from new users by each method. The main reason that the random selection does not perform well is that it chooses items that will not be rated by new users. The probability that the random selection receives a rating is less that 0.01. When the new user does not rate the queried item, that new user is moved to the unknown child node. As the predictions in the unknown child node do not significantly differ from the predictions at the current node, this strategy is not able to improve the accuracy of predictions. Remember that test users and training users have the same distributions. If test (new) users do not know the split item, training users do not know it either. Therefore, decision trees which are built using training users with the random selection strategy are very imbalanced. This means that almost all users of the current node are moved to the unknown child node and consequently the predictions at the current node and the child nodes would be almost the same. LMP and GMP receive more ratings compared to the random selection, that is why their performance also improves in Figure 7.3.

As Bootstrapping and FDT rely on the same decision tree, they have the same probabilities in Table 7.1. Interestingly, Bootstrapping (or FDT) receives less ratings compare to GMP and almost the same number compared to LMP, but its performance is better than that of the others. This evidence shows that receiving ratings from the new user is not the only important factor in performance. The rating should also be informative, i.e. effective in reducing the test error. Bootstrapping takes this into account by computing the error at child nodes and picking the item that has minimum error. Ignoring this fact and opting solely for asking items that new users are able to give ratings to them, will not result in good performance.

Table 7.1: The probability that the new user likes the queried item (p_{like}), dislikes it ($p_{dislike}$), or does not rate it ($p_{unknown}$) for different active learning methods.

Method	p_{like}	$p_{dislike}$	$p_{unknown}$
Random	0.004	0.003	0.993
LMP	0.18	0.16	0.66
GMP	0.26	0.17	0.57
Bootstrapping and FDT	0.18	0.15	0.67

Coming back to Figure 7.3, FDT and Bootstrapping methods start with the same initial error because, as was already pointed out, FDT uses the item average for rating prediction at the root of the tree. In the first query, Bootstrapping and FDT are more or less equal. This is because there are only 3 pseudo users in the first level. The superiority of MF against the nearest neighbor is more obvious when MF is trained with many users. As we go down to the lower levels, the number of pseudo users increases and the benefit of rating prediction with MF also becomes more clear. After 8 queries, the amount of improvement is 0.005, which is significant in the Netflix dataset. As asking more queries would not significantly improve FDT, we stop active learning in this step.

In addition to improving accuracy, FDT provides user and item features that can be exploited for other purposes besides the cold-start recommendation. Such information is not provided in (Golbandi *et al.*, 2011) since they only build decision trees that contain the predictions (item average) and the split items of the nodes. From this point of view, we can compare our approach to (Zhou *et al.*, 2011). While both methods give us user and item features at the end of the learning phase, our approach is much more scalable. Note that the scalability is an important factor because the Netflix dataset is not the largest recommendation dataset. Yahoo Music[1] contains 717 M ratings, so it is more than 7 times bigger than the Netflix dataset. Therefore, we need to think about the scalability of our approaches.

Table 7.2: Hyper-parameters of FDT in all levels

level	α	λ
1	0.0013	0.001
2	0.0013	0.001
3	0.001	0.001
4	0.0012	0.003
5	0.0012	0.003
6	0.0013	0.01
7	0.0015	0.01
8	0.0006	0.02

A grid search methodology was followed to find hyper-parameters. The hyper-parameters of each level are reported in table 7.2. In our experiments, varying k did not change the results, so we fixed it to 70. Also, the best value of γ was 0.0001 for all trees.

Even a small lift in RMSE leads to significant financial benefit for companies (Koren, 2007). As a result, the improvements achieved are relevant. The same observation is made in the related works even for smaller datasets (Harpale & Yang, 2008; Jin & Si, 2004) or for similar problems, e.g. a recent paper (Chen *et al.*, 2013) as the problem is difficult: there are many candidate items to ask their ratings from new users but new users are willing to rate just a few of them. Moreover, we start without any ratings from the new user, which makes the problem more severe.

Now we go on to show the results of MPS. We do not use MF in this part and the decision trees are constructed according to (Golbandi *et al.*, 2011). However, to expand the nodes, only a subset of all candidate items are checked based on MPS. Tables 7.3 and 7.4 show the speed and the accuracy of MPS in different sampling sizes and queries respectively.

It is clear that MPS does not adversely affect the accuracy at all while speeding up the tree construction algorithm by one order of magnitude. This observation shows that the best items to query are among popular items and non-popular items are irrelevant. To understand why this happens, we should see the rating frequencies of the items. Figure 7.4 shows the distribution of items' rating frequencies in the Netflix dataset.

[1] http://webscope.sandbox.yahoo.com/catalog.php?datatype=r

Table 7.3: Running time for different sampling size. The running time is in hours:minute format

#samples	time (hours:min)
17770	**119:54**
1000	**12:30**
200	**04:25**

Table 7.4: RMSE for different sampling size

#	ini. query	query 1	query 2	query 3	query 4	query 5	query 6	query 7	query 8	query 9	query 10
17770	0.9872	0.9784	0.9718	0.9661	0.9620	0.9589	0.9568	0.9555	0.9546	0.9540	0.9537
1000	0.9872	0.9784	0.9718	0.9661	0.9620	0.9589	0.9568	0.9555	0.9546	0.9540	0.9537
200	0.9872	0.9784	0.9718	0.9658	0.9618	0.9587	0.9567	0.9553	0.9545	0.9539	0.9536

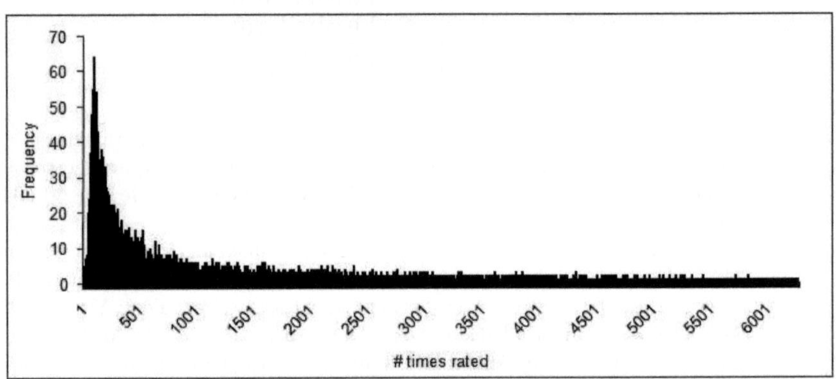

Figure 7.4: Distribution of items' rating frequency in the Netflix dataset

According to this distribution, most of the items have received less than 1000 ratings. Therefore, splitting users with a non-popular item will move most of the users to the "Unknown" child node and, as it was discussed in section 7.5.1, recommender systems gain nothing. However, splitting the nodes with popular items distributes the users of the current among the child nodes in a way that there are enough users at child nodes to provide accurate predictions. For example, in the case of the first selected item, 49461 users like it, 29913 users dislike it and 280767 do not rate it. As there are enough users in the "Like" and "Dislike" nodes and the number of "Unknown" users is much lower than the current node, the new predictions are significantly different from the current node's predictions, leading to significant improvement in new predictions.

Table 7.5: The popularity ranking of the selected items

#query	average	min	max
1	136	136	136
2	56.6	36	96
3	172.4	3	326
4	495.8	9	9759
5	324.3	1	7029
6	544.9	1	17770
7	760.1	2	17770
8	520.6	1	17770
9	1327.8	1	17770
10	2564.8	1	17770

Table 7.5 provides more insights into why sampling popular items works. The average, the minimum and the maximum popularity rankings of the selected items for each query are shown in this table. In the first query, all three rankings are the same because we need to select only one item for the root of the tree. The max ranking increases from level two on and eventually in the last five levels becomes 17770, which is the maximum ranking. This shows that the best split item may not exist among the sampled items of some nodes in some layers, though its effect is not significant according to the table 7.4. Also, the min ranking is one on many levels, meaning on those levels there are nodes whose best split item is the local most popular, though according to the Figure 7.3, such nodes are few because LMP does not perform well.

The best method for analyzing Table 7.4 is average ranking. In the initial queries, the average ranking is rather small. As we go to the lower levels, the ranking also increases. On some levels, the average ranking is larger than 200 or 1000. One could expect that on those levels, the sampling would be detrimental to the accuracy. However, the results in Table 7.4 show that this is not the case and we can simply ignore items whose ranking is larger than 200 or 1000. Surprisingly, sampling 200 items even slightly improves the accuracy after 2 queries. To understand the reason for this evidence, the learning algorithm of decision trees should be taken into account. Decision trees are built by choosing the items that minimize training error. But those items do not necessarily minimize test error as well. Therefore, it makes sense to ignore some items that lead to smaller training error, when we are unsure about their test error. The results show that items that are very popular pose lower uncertainty with respect to their test error.

The third part of this section deals with the 6-way split. Like the 3-way split, ratings can be predicted based on the item average or FDT. Figure 7.5 shows the

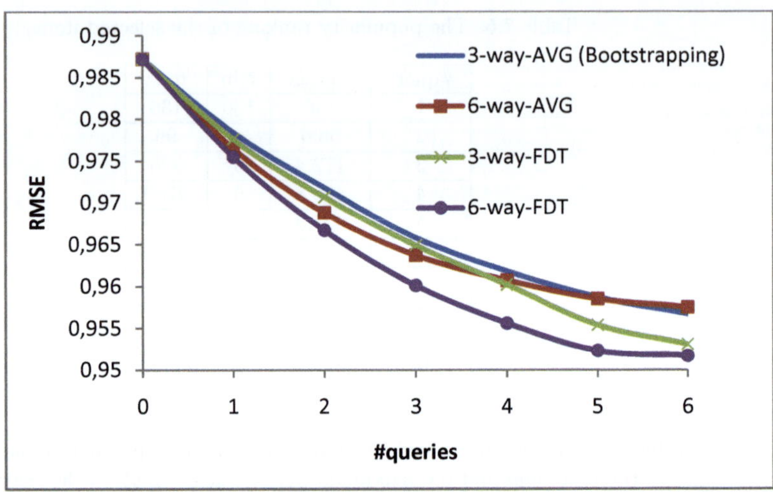

Figure 7.5: RMSE results of 6-way split based on FDT (6-way-FDT), 6-way split based on item average (6-way-AVG), 3-way split based on FDT (3-way-FDT), and 3-way-AVG (Bootstrapping).

results of the 6-way split based on the item average (6-way-AVG), the 6-way split based on the FDT (6-way-FDT), the 3-way split based on the FDT (3-way-FDT), and Bootstrapping. All results are based on the MPS where the sampling size is 200. The hyper-parameters of 6-way-FDT are reported in Table 7.8. As we expected the 6-way-AVG beats Bootstrapping because it provides more refined splits. 6-way-FDT further improves the 6-way-AVG since it leverages MF for rating prediction. The benefit of using MF for rating prediction instead of the item average is more clear in the 6-way split compared to the 3-way split. The reason is that the accuracy we gain at each level is the summation of the improvements of all users at the corresponding level. The higher the number of users, the larger the improvement.

After 5 queries, 6-way-AVG converges to Bootstrapping (3-way-AVG) and even starts to become worse with the sixth query. This happens because, as we go down to the deeper layers of decision trees, the number of associated users of nodes drops. Therefore, the ratings in such nodes are predicted with less training data, which obviously adversely affects accuracy. Although the predictions are still regularized towards the predictions in the parent node, this regularization might not be enough to compensate for the effect of less training data in such nodes. However, 6-way-FDT does not suffer from this problem because it does not use hierarchical regularization, instead it exploits typical ℓ_2 regularization.

Table 7.6: Hyper-parameters of 6-way-FDT in all levels

level	α	λ
1	0.0011	0.016
2	0.0015	0.007
3	0.0013	0.005
4	0.0013	0.005
5	0.0013	0.009
6	0.0004	0.03

The benefit of the 6-way split becomes more clear for datasets whose range of ratings is more refined. For example, in EachMovie[1], the range of ratings is from one to six, or in IMDb[2], it is from one to ten. It is expected that the amount of improvement in 6-way-FDT would be larger in those datasets.

As the results of Figure 7.5 show, going beyond query 6 is not beneficial for 6-way-FDT. For 3-way-FDT and 3-way-AVG, this convergence happens after 8 and 10 queries, respectively. In general, decision trees would not help too much after a specific level where the number of nodes exceeds a threshold. And this threshold depends on the way that the nodes are split (3-way or 6-way) and the predictive models (MF or item average). But remember that our goal is to reach this convergence with minimum queries, because new users are not willing to answer many questions. For the same reason, we use active learning in machine learning, i.e. to train a good model with the minimum queries. If we wanted to ask many queries, all active learning methods would exhibit the same performance at the end.

The last experimental results in this section report the performance of the warm FDT. Table 7.7 compares the 6-way-FDT with the warm 6-way-FDT. The warm FDT is also based on the 6-way split, but to train MF, the user and item features are initialized as was explained in section 7.5.3.

Table 7.7: RMSE results of warm FDT and FDT

method	ini query	query 1	query 2	query 3	query 4	query 5	query 6
6-way-FDT	0.9872	0.9755	0.9667	0.9601	0.9555	0.9523	0.9517
warm 6-way-FDT	0.9872	0.9755	0.9662	0.9596	0.9551	0.9519	0.9518

We cannot apply the warm 6-way-FDT method in the first level because there is no MF at the root level. Therefore, the RMSE is the same for both methods after the first query. In the next queries, warm 6-way-FDT slightly improves 6-way-FDT, though the

[1] http://grouplens.org/datasets/eachmovie/
[2] http://www.imdb.com/interfaces

amount of improvement is not too much. We leave other methods for initialization as the future work.

Table 7.8: Hyper-parameters of warm 6-way-FDT in all levels

level	α	λ
1	0.0013	0.016
2	0.0009	0.003
3	0.0009	0.003
4	0.0009	0.005
5	0.001	0.009
6	0.0004	0.038

7.6.3 Comparing Online Updating and Item Average

In chapters 6 and 5, we relied on online updating to learn new user features. The features are initially learned with three random seeds and then they are updated after receiving new ratings from the new user. The idea of starting with three ratings had been proposed in (Harpale & Yang, 2008; Jin & Si, 2004). This assumption is necessary because otherwise the new user features are initialized randomly and consequently the predictions for the new user would also be random. However, this assumption is not realistic when we are dealing with a new user who has not rated any item (which is the problem we are studying). Besides not being realistic, online updating performs poorly compared to the item average, given that the number of ratings for the new user is only a few.

Table 7.9 shows the RMSE of applying most popular item selection, given online updating is used. Compared to the most popular active learning for decision trees (Figure 7.3), online updating loses with a large margin. The initial error in online updating is 1.0560, which is much larger than the item average (0.9872). This gap cannot be compensated for in the next queries. So, we can conclude that online updating is not a suitable approach for the new user problem in recommender systems because new users eventually provide a few ratings, which is not enough to train accurate user features. To exploit the power of MF, other approaches should be taken into account. In this chapter, we proposed a FDT in this regard, and the results confirmed the success of our approach.

7.7 Summary and Future Work

The main challenge of the new user problem in recommender systems is how to incorporate recommendation techniques of active (warm) users into new users. Although matrix factorization is the state-of-the-art predictive model for recommender systems

Table 7.9: The accuracy of the most popular active learning for MF in the first three queries. MF is retrained using the online updating technique.

ini. query	query 1	query 2	query 3
1.056	1.0395	1.0295	1.0234

since the Netflix prize, the way that it should be leveraged for new users is not trivial. In this chapter, we proposed a framework to use MF in this regard. The framework is based on decision trees, which has been proposed by (Golbandi *et al.*, 2011). Their motivation is to adapt the interview process to new users' responses to queries. In general, this approach is the right approach to address the new user problem. But they use item average for rating prediction, which is simple. As MF is a superior model for recommender systems, it makes a lot of sense to use it for new users as well. In this chapter, we proposed FDT to incorporate MF into decision trees. The FDT constructs decision trees like Bootstrapping (Golbandi *et al.*, 2011) and then trains an MF model for the last level of decision trees. In this way, building decision trees is tractable and also the predictions are more accurate. Moreover, we proposed Warm FDT, in which user and item features of MF are initialized with user and item features of the MF model for the previous level. Therefore, Warm FDT builds two decision trees, one with the depth N and one with depth $N-1$.

We proposed MPS to speed up tree construction. MPS only investigates the items that are the most popular among users associated with the nodes. The results show that MPS makes the tree construction algorithm much faster without adversely affecting the accuracy.

In (Golbandi *et al.*, 2011), the nodes of decision trees are split in a 3-way fashion, meaning ratings one, two, and three are not distinguished, the same for the ratings four and five. The reason that Bootstrapping opts for a 3-way split is to save running time because it is slow. However, MPS is already able to cope with the speed problem, so given MPS, one could go for a 6-way split. The results show that the 6-way split outperforms the 3-way split, especially if it is combined with FDT.

As future work, we can replace decision trees with a graph. The drawback of decision trees is that each user appears only in one node and consequently does not affect the predictions in the other nodes. This drawback can be fixed by replacing decision trees with weighted graphs. The weights show how similar the nodes are. The rating prediction at the nodes are the results of the local prediction at the nodes and the weighted summation of the predictions at the other nodes.

FDT relies on the same tree, constructed by Bootstrapping, and does not exploit MF to build trees because it becomes very complicated. However, we can fix this problem by developing a new fold-in method. In this method, to measure the test error of pool items, we fold-in 3 (or 6 in a 6-way split) pseudo users into the MF model of the previous layer in which user features of these pseudo users are initialized with the user features of their parent node. Then, using the online updating technique, we retrain their user features. As user features are hopefully initialized close to their final values and only those features are retrained, it is expected that the retraining would quickly converge. Therefore, finding the best split item is tractable and feasible. In this way, the trees built would be different from Bootstrapping and hopefully more accurate.

In this chapter, we showed that a 6-way split improves the 3-way split in the first queries, but after 5 queries they converge to the same point. Perhaps this happens because of the poor regularization in the deeper layers of 6-way trees. However, regardless of the regularization, this evidence shows that the 6-way split is not always better than the 3-way split. Therefore, we can opt for trees whose number of splits is not fixed. This means nodes can be split in different ways, i.e. 2-way, 3-way, 4-way, 5-way, and 6-way. The right choice depends on the node. All possibilities are checked and the best way of splitting, i.e. the one that leads to less error, is selected. Note that in this approach regardless of the number of splitting ways, one child node is dedicated to the "Unknown" answer and the rest of the child nodes can take one or more ratings if the ratings assigned to each node are continuous. For example, in the 3-way splitting tree, ratings 1 to 4 can be assigned to the first child node, rating 5 to the second child node and "Unknown" to the last node. Another possibility is to assign ratings 1 to 3 to the first child node, rating 4 and 5 to the second, and unknown to the last child node. In total, there are 4 different rating assignments for 3-way splitting trees. Note that an assignment like 1, 3, and 4 to a child node is not allowed. It should be mentioned that building decision trees with a flexible number of splits is more expensive, too. There are three things that must be checked in each node: the right number of splits, the right assignment of ratings to nodes, and the right item to split. Taking all three factors into consideration, the learning algorithm will be slow.

In this chapter, we clarified the difference between decision trees and the decision process. We mentioned that as our work trees are used to find item predictions in the leaf nodes, trees are in fact multivariate (vector-value target) regression trees. One approach to extend our work is to remove rating predictions at child nodes and use trees as decision processes. The decisions would be the right item to query from new users. Furthermore, if we add the Markov property to the nodes, we would have a Markov Decision Process (MDP). In this case, we can apply Reinforcement Learning (RL) to learn this decision process. We can define actions as items for querying, reward as the amount of error reduction, and state as the combination of queried items and their answers. However, we should be careful because in this way the number of states and actions would be high, which may require longer training time. Therefore, we should limit the number of potential items for query by MPS and also replace ratings 1 to 5 with "Like" and "Dislike" answers.

Although warm FDT proposed in this chapter could slightly improve FDT, the improvements were not significant. Therefore, it would be interesting to work on other methods to exploit the initial knowledge we have learned from the previous level into the MF of the next level. For example, instead of initializing user features with the features of the parent node, the features could be *regularized* towards the parent's node features. Item features can also be regularized towards the item features of the previous level.

An interesting observation that we reported in this chapter was the comparison between online updating and item average. We showed that the item average outperforms online updating with a large margin. This observation can help us to develop a new learning algorithm for MF in general, i.e. not especially for new users. The fact that online updating performs poorly for new users means that MF is not able to provide accurate predictions for users or items with a few ratings. The ratings of such users can be improved by item average. Therefore, we can incorporate the item average into MF to improve the predictions for items or users who do not have many ratings.

In this chapter, we used decision trees for rating prediction. We can also use them for item recommendation. In this case, we need to design a new learning algorithm to learn decision trees. This algorithm uses an objective function that is defined on the basis of item recommendation measures instead of RMSE.

Chapter 8

Learning Active Learning

Active learning for the new user problem in recommender systems is different from active learning in classification (regression) because although there is no data for new users, there is abundant data for active (training) users. In chapters 5 and 6, we exploited this additional data to define uncertainty measures for the aspect model and matrix factorization. In this chapter, we want to use this data in a more efficient way.

8.1 General Framework

In general, the goal of active learning is to choose examples for query that will reduce test error as much as possible when the predictive model is retrained with their labels. There are two difficulties in reaching this goal. First, the test data is missing. Moreover, the labels are not known before asking the queries, so even if the test data is available, it is not possible to retrain the model and measure the new test error because the labels are missing.

The same problems exist for active learning in recommender systems as well. There is no test data for new users and their ratings are unknown before asking the queries. But in recommender systems there is additional data that does not exist in the classification problem: there are already many training (active) users. We can consider each training user as an (artificial) new user, separate part of these ratings as the test data, and put the rest of the ratings in the pool data. Then, we can compute the effect of each pool item on test error, because the ratings of the pool items are known and the test data is also available. In the end, we know the error reduction of all items for the target training user, so we can choose the best item, which is the one with maximum error reduction. Now we can claim that we have solved the active learning problem for this specific user.

The same procedure can be done for other training users to learn their active learning problems. After solving all active learning problems for training users, we should aggregate this knowledge to identify the best item to be asked of a real new user. In fact, each solved active learning problem acts like an instance. The set of instances gives us a training data set which can be used to learn the process behind them and this process is active learning for the new user problem in recommender systems. That is why we call this approach *Learning Active Learning* (LAL).

Algorithm 10 describes the general framework of LAL. For each training user, first the ratings are split into pool and test data. Note that the pool data contains all items, including those whose ratings are missing. Like the previous chapter, our settings allow new users not to rate the queried items, so items with missing values should also be included in the pool data. Obviously, those items do not have any impact on test error because they cannot improve the predictive model.

Algorithm 10 The General Algorithm of Learning Active Learning (LAL)

Input: $\mathcal{D}^{\text{train}}$
Output: i^*

for $u \in U(\mathcal{D}^{\text{train}})$ **do**
  split $\mathcal{D}_u^{\text{train}}$ into $\mathcal{D}_u^{\text{pool}}$ and $\mathcal{D}_u^{\text{test}}$
  $\mathcal{D}_u^{\text{pool}} = \mathcal{D}_u^{\text{pool}} \cup \{(u, i, .) | i \in I, i \notin \mathcal{D}_u^{\text{pool}}\}$
  for $i \in \mathcal{D}_u^{\text{pool}}$ **do**
    $\Delta_{ui} = RMSE_u^1 - RMSE_u^2$
  end for
end for
$\bar{\delta} = aggregate\_function(\Delta_{ui})$
$max = -\infty$
$i^* = -1$
for $i \in I$ **do**
  if $\bar{\delta}_i > max$ **then**
    $max = \bar{\delta}_i$
    $i^* = i$
  end if
end for

There are several possibilities to compute the effect of the pool data on test error. For example, we can train the model with all pool data except for the candidate item and measure the test error. Then we again train the model with all pool data including the candidate item and measure the new test error. The difference between the new and the old test error indicates how much the candidate item can reduce the test error. We call this difference Δ. Another possibility is to measure the first error by random initialization of the model parameters and then train the model with only the candidate item to measure the new error. In this way, it would be faster to compute Δ because it trains the model only once while the former method requires training the model twice. However, it might be less accurate because the new error is based on only one rating. To measure the error, we use $RMSE$ (see section 2.3). $RMSE_u^1$ denotes the test error of user u before adding the candidate item to the training data and $RMSE_u^2$ denotes the test error afterwards. After computing Δ_{ui} for all users and items, we need to aggregate them to know eventually which item is the best item for query. In fact, the aggregation step is like a function that its inputs are the solved *active learning* problems, and the task of this function is to process these inputs to *learn* the expected error reduction of items, which is the aim of active learning. In the end, after learning the expected error reduction of all items, we choose the item that has the maximum error reduction.

There are several possibilities for aggregation. For example, we can compute the average Δ of each item over all users and choose the item that has the maximum average. Another possibility is to count how many times an item has been the best item in each separate active learning problem for training users and choose the item with the maximum occurrence. The average aggregation function is described in algorithm 11. The output of the algorithm is $\bar{\delta}$, which is a vector storing the average error reduction of all items. The best item i^* is the item with the maximum $\bar{\delta}_{i^*}$.

Algorithm 11 The algorithm of average aggregation function

Input: Δ , U, I
Output: $\bar{\delta}$

for $i \in I$ **do**
  $\bar{\delta}_i = 0$
  for $u \in U$ **do**
    $\bar{\delta}_i = \bar{\delta}_i + \bar{\Delta}_{ui}$
  end for
  $\bar{\delta}_i = \bar{\delta}_i / |U|$
end for

Algorithm 10 finds only one query. If N queries are going to be asked, we need to find N items. A trivial solution would be to rank items according to their δ_i in descending order and then pick the top N items. However, recent research indicates that selecting a fixed set of items upfront and asking them one by one is not a good strategy (Golbandi *et al.*, 2011; Rashid *et al.*, 2008). Rather, it would be better to adapt the interview process according to the new users' answers to the previous queries. To change the algorithm 10 based on this point, we propose the following: after finding the first query and getting its answer from the new user, a subset of $\mathcal{D}^{\text{train}}$ who have the same answer to the queried items are found. To find the second query, Δ in algorithm 10 is computed only based on this subset of users and not on all $\mathcal{D}^{\text{train}}$. In this way, the LAL algorithm adapts itself to the new user preferences by computing Δ with users who are similar to the new user. In principle, this is similar to collaborative filtering. In collaborative filtering, the unknown ratings are computed based on the ratings of similar users. In this work, instead of using the ratings of similar users for *rating prediction*, we employ those ratings for *query prediction*.

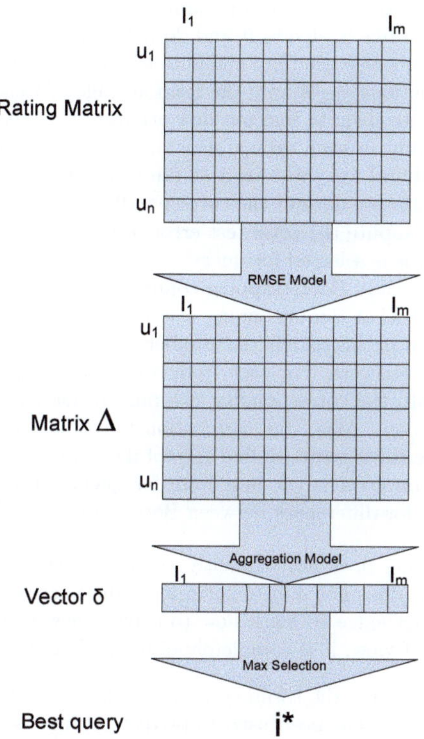

Figure 8.1: A schematic view of LAL stages

8.2 Learning Active Learning Using Decision Trees

The general framework of LAL relies on a model to generate Δ and then aggregate them to learn δ. In this section, we would like to implement this approach using decision trees, which has been proposed by (Golbandi *et al.*, 2011) and was already discussed in chapter 7. Like chapter 7, we call (Golbandi *et al.*, 2011) *Bootstrapping.*

The reason for choosing Bootstrapping is that it is close to the idea of LAL. First, let's have another look at Bootstrapping from the LAL point of view. There is an item and we do not know how good this item is to query to the new user because its rating is not known upfront. However, there are already many training users and their ratings are available. So, instead of trying to find out how good the item is for the new user, we investigate how good this item is for training users. The training users are divided into groups: those who *like* it, *dislike* it and do not know it (*unknown*). We treat the users of each group as a single user and compute the same rating predictions for all of them. The rating predictions are simply the item average. After computing the predictions, we need to evaluate them to find out how accurate the predictions are. The evaluation is done individually in each group. For that, all ratings of the corresponding users' group are unified and are considered as the test data. The test error of each group is the RMSE over all test data of the corresponding group. Finally, three test errors are summed up to compute the total test error of the candidate item. The item that has the minimum error is selected for query.

If we want to study Bootstrapping compared to the general framework of LAL, we can say that somewhat Bootstrapping also builds an error matrix E that is similar to the matrix Δ. But in this matrix the number of users (rows) is just three, corresponding to three possible answers. For each item, we find the square error of the child nodes and put them into the corresponding column. In fact, the matrix is filled out in the column-wise fashion. Also, the aggregation function is a summation operator which sums up over the three errors to find the total error of each item. In the end, the item with the minimum error is the best item for query. However, despite this similarity, there are two major differences between Bootstrapping and LAL:

1. Bootstrapping does not explicitly treat each training user as an artificial new user. So, it does not aim to solve individual active learning problems and then use this knowledge to learn how to solve a new problem for a new user. From this point of view, it is completely different from the approach of LAL.

2. In Bootstrapping, the training data and the test data are the same. Namely, the same data that has been used to predict ratings using the item average method is also used for evaluation. Again, this is not what LAL does. In LAL, the test data does not appear in the pool data, so they are not used in training data.

Now we want to fix the above issues and propose a new learning algorithm for decision trees that is consistent with the framework of LAL. In our approach, like Bootstrapping, the rating predictions for nodes are done using the item average. However, instead of the 3-way split in Bootstrapping, we use a 6-way split. There is one child node per each possible rating from 1 to 5 plus a child node for the missing rating. Algorithm 12 describes the details of this learning algorithm.

Suppose we are at node t and we are going to ask q-th query, which must be selected from I^{pool}. First, we split the ratings of associated users U^t to pool and test. $\mathcal{D}^t$ contains the ratings of all associated users of node t. Then, we compute the rating predictions of all pool items I^{pool} using the item average. After computing the predictions, we can compute the current test error of the users. Now we go on to find out how much each pool item can reduce the test error. Each pool item splits the node into 6 child nodes.

Algorithm 12 LAL based on decision trees

ConstructDecisionTree
Input: $\mathcal{D}^t$, I^{pool},q
Output: i^*

for $u \in U^t$ **do**
  split $\mathcal{D}^t_u$ into $\mathcal{D}^{\text{pool}}_u$ and $\mathcal{D}^{\text{test}}_u$
  $\mathcal{D}^{\text{pool}}_u = \mathcal{D}^{\text{pool}}_u \cup \{(u, i, .)|i \in I, i \notin \mathcal{D}^{\text{pool}}_u\}$
end for
for $i \in I^{pool}$ **do**
  compute $\hat{r}_{ti}$ using item average (Equation 4.12)
end for
for $u \in U^t$ **do**
  compute $RMSE^1_u$
end for
for $i \in I^{pool}$ **do**
  split U^t into 6 child nodes according to their ratings to item i
  for each child node v **do**
    compute $\hat{r}_{vi}$ using item average (Equation 4.12)
  end for
  for $u \in U_t$ **do**
    find the child node v that user u has move there
    compute $RMSE^2_u$ based on the new predictions in the child node v
    $\Delta_{ui} = RMSE^1_u - RMSE^2_u$
  end for
end for
$\bar{\delta} = aggregate\_function(\Delta_{ui})$
$max = -\infty$
$i^* = -1$
for $i \in I^{pool}$ **do**
  if $\bar{\delta}_i > max$ **then**
    $max = \bar{\delta}_i$
    $i^* = i$
  end if
end for
if $q < N$ **and** $\bar{\Delta}_{i^*} \geq 0$ **then**
  create 6 child nodes based on the selected item i^*
  $I^{pool}_{new} = I^{pool}/i^*$
  for child node v **do**
    recursively call ConstructDecisionTree ($\mathcal{D}^v$,$I^{pool}_{new}, q + 1$)
  end for
end if

In the child nodes, the rating predictions are again computed using item average. To compute the new $RMSE$ of user u, first we need to find the child node v to which user u has moved. $RMSE_u^2$ is computed with the new predictions at the child node v. Then Δ_{ui} is computed, which is the difference between the initial $RMSE_u^1$ and the new one $RMSE_u^2$. After finding all Δ_{ui}, we aggregate them using the average aggregation function (Algorithm 11). The item that has the maximum δ_{i^*} is selected for query. After finding the best query i^*, we go on to find the next best queries. So, we create child nodes using i^* and recursively call the ConstructDecisionTree function to split these nodes. Now we need to avoid selecting one item twice, so i^* is removed from the pool items of the child nodes.

There are two stopping criteria. First, if the number of queries that we have asked so far q is equal to the maximum number of queries that we are supposed to ask N. The second criterion is about δ_{i^*}. In most of the cases, as we expected, δ_{i^*} is positive. This means that splitting nodes will result in a more coherent cluster of users, which consequently improves accuracy. However, sometimes this does not happen and there is no item that splitting the current node with it, would improve the accuracy of the predictions of the current node. In such cases, δ_{i^*} is negative. One reason for this phenomenon is that as we go down into the deep layers of the decision trees, the number of associated users of nodes decreases. Therefore, the ratings in such nodes are predicted with less training data, which obviously adversely affects the accuracy. Although the predictions are still regularized towards the predictions in the parent node, this regularization might not be enough to compensate for the effect of less training data in such nodes. In the case of negative δ_{i^*}, the current node is not split any further.

In chapter 7, we showed that rating predictions in the leaf nodes of decision trees can be improved by FDT. We also proposed warm FDT, which takes advantage of the initialization of MF parameters using the parameters MF for trees with a lesser number of queries. We can apply these methods in the decision trees that are built by LAL as well. In this way, we can benefit from the right strategy for active learning and also the right predictive model for rating prediction. In the experiment, we will refer to these methods as LAL-FDT and LAL-Warm-FDT. Also, LAL-AVG refers to LAL whose ratings are predicted with item average.

8.3 Experimental Results

8.3.1 Experimental Setup

In this section, we experimentally examine the performance of LAL. Our objective is to investigate the accuracy of rating prediction with respect to the number of queries asked to new users. It is important to obtain improvement in accuracy after a small number of queries, since users are generally reluctant to answer many of such queries.

As (Golbandi *et al.*, 2011) conducted their experiment on the Netflix dataset, we also ran our experiments on this dataset. In chapter 2, we mentioned how this dataset was split into four datasets: train, validation, pool and test. The validation dataset was used for two purposes in our experiments. First, to find the hyper-parameters of MF in FDT. Second, as the test data of artificial new users ($\mathcal{D}_u^{\text{test}}$). We picked the 6-way-FDT and the 6-way-AVG as the baseline for comparison purposes. These methods have already been explained in chapter 7. First, we will report the results of LAL-FDT and LAL-AVG and then we will finish this section by showing the results of LAL-Warm-FDT.

8.3.2 Results

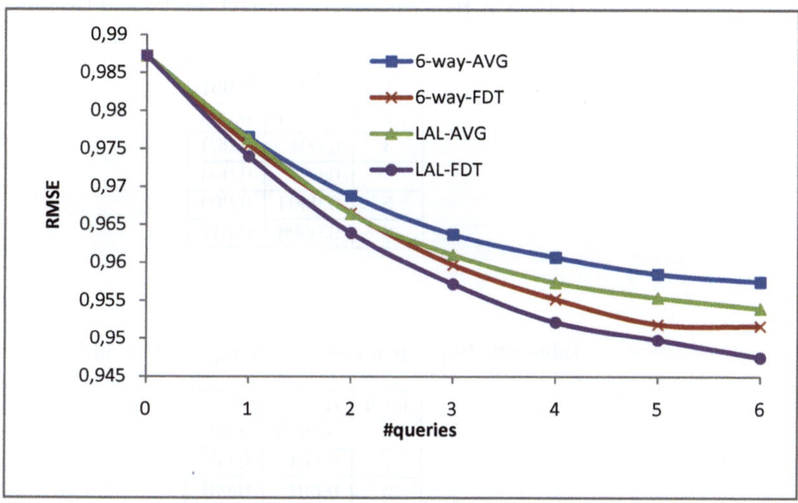

Figure 8.2: RMSE results of LAL, 6-way-FDT, and 6-way-AVG. LAL is tested on two prediction models: the item average (LAL-AVG) and matrix factorization (LAL-FDT)

Figure 8.2 shows the results of LAL-FDT, LAL-AVG, 6-way-FDT and 6-way-AVG. First, we compared LAL-FDT to 6-way-FDT to find out how learning active learning works given the best prediction model, i.e. MF is used. Clearly, LAL-FDT outperforms in all queries. The same fact is also confirmed when we compare LAL-AVG to 6-way-AVG. Therefore, regardless of the prediction model, LAL outperforms the 6-way split. This happens because in LAL the test data that is used to evaluate the split items is different from the training data that is used for rating prediction, but in the 6-way split they are the same. Moreover, in LAL each training user is treated as as an artificial new user and in the end, using all artificial new users, we learn how to solve the active learning problem for a real new user.

Interestingly, the 6-way-FDT outperforms LAL-AVG. It shows that the power of MF in FDT can compensate for the weakness of the active learning strategy in the 6-way split. As going on after six queries does not significantly improve the RMSE of LAL-FDT and 6-way-FDT, the tree construction algorithm stops there. The reason for this convergence was already discussed in the experimental section of chapter 7.

A grid search methodology was followed to find hyper-parameters for LAL-MF. The hyper-parameters of each level are reported in table 8.1. In our experiments, varying k did not change the results, so we fixed it to 70. Also, the best value of γ was 0.0001 for all levels. The hyper-parameters of 6-way-FDT are reported in table 8.2.

Table 8.1: Hyper-parameters of LAL-FDT in all levels

level	α	λ
1	0.001	0.001
2	0.0013	0.005
3	0.001	0.003
4	0.001	0.003
5	0.0004	0.009
6	0.0006	0.017

Table 8.2: Hyper-parameters of 6-way-FDT in all levels

level	α	λ
1	0.0013	0.001
2	0.0013	0.001
3	0.001	0.001
4	0.0012	0.003
5	0.0012	0.003
6	0.0013	0.01

The regularization factor is small in the first levels and increases as we go to the lower levels. The reason is that in the first levels, all the training data has been partitioned into a few pseudo users. As a result, there is a lot of training data for each pseudo user. But in the lower levels, the number of pseudo users increases while the number of the ratings for each of them decreases. Therefore, to avoid over-fitting, more regularization is needed.

In the last part of this section, we report the results of LAL-Warm-FDT. Table 8.3 shows LAL-FDT versus LAL-Warm-FDT. We cannot apply the LAL-Warm-FDT method in the first level because there is no MF in the root of decision trees.

Table 8.3: RMSE results of LAL-FDT and LAL-Warm-FDT

method	ini. query	query 1	query 2	query 3	query 4	query 5	query 6
LAL-FDT	0.9872	0.9740	0.9639	0.9572	0.9522	0.9498	0.9475
LAL-Warm-FDT	0.9872	0.9740	0.9637	0.9567	0.9517	0.9489	0.9474

Therefore, the RMSE is the same for both methods after the first query. In the next queries, LAL-Warm-FDT slightly improves LAL-FDT though the amount of improvement is not significant. We leave other methods for initialization as future work.

Table 8.4: Hyper-parameters of LAL-Warm-FDT in all levels

level	α	λ
1	0.001	0.001
2	0.0008	0.001
3	0.0008	0.003
4	0.0008	0.004
5	0.0004	0.014
6	0.0005	0.017

8.4 Summary and Future Work

Compared to the application of active learning in classification (regression), active learning in recommender systems presents several differences. The reason is that although there are no ratings for new users, an abundance of available ratings already exists –collectively– from past users. In this paper, we propose an innovative approach for active learning in recommender systems, which aims at taking advantage of this additional information. The main idea is to consider past users as (artificial) new users in order to learn the right queries to be asked to new users for active-learning purposes. In fact, each active learning problem solved acts like an instance. The set of instances gives us a training data set, which can be used to learn the process behind them and this process is the active learning problem for the new user problem in recommender systems. That is why we call this approach *learning active learning.* Based on this framework, we investigated two different types of models: the first model is based on information about average item ratings and the second on FDT, which was introduced in chapter 7. The results on the Netflix dataset indicate that the best improvement is achieved when LAL is combined with FDT. It enjoys the right active learning strategy (LAL) and a strong predictive model (MF). This combination can beat LAL without FDT (i.e. LAL-AVG) and FDT without LAL (i.e. 6-way-FDT). Finally, warm FDT can slightly improve the accuracy of LAL-FDT.

LAL relies on two models. The first model is used to measure the test error of training users to generate matrix $\Delta^{U \times I}$ and the second model aggregates this matrix into a vector δ^I containing the overall error reduction of items. In this work, we used decision trees to generate matrix Δ and δ was obtained by taking the average over all observed Δ_{ui} for each item. There are several ways to extend our work by changing these models. We can use other models besides decision trees to generate matrix Δ . It would also be interesting to use other aggregation models, for example a counting model that counts how many times an item has been selected as the best item for training users and chooses the one with the maximum number of occurrences.

In the future work of chapter 7, we mentioned the idea of using decision trees for item recommendation and not rating prediction. The same approach can also be applied in LAL as well. This means the objective function of the learning algorithm is changed in a way that optimizes the accuracy of item recommendation instead of rating prediction. In this case, the matrix Δ shows the amount of improvement in item recommendation, before and after incorporating items in the training data. After the aggregation, the item with the maximum improvement is selected for query.

As users usually give ratings to few items, $\mathcal{D}_u^{\text{pool}}$ contains few rated items (u, i, r) and many unrated items $(u, i, .)$. Therefore, matrix Δ is sparse since items without ratings cannot be evaluated on the test data. We did not address this sparsity in our work. As future work, one could think of predicting the missing values of Δ and aggregate the dense matrix $\hat{\Delta}$ to find the best item. Obviously, MF is the superior technique to be exploited for this purpose.

Chapter 9

Active Learning for Museum Recommender Systems

In this chapter, we will discuss how active learning can be used for recommender systems in museums. In fact, this chapter shows how the theoretical achievements of this thesis can help us to overcome the difficulties that exist in real applications. As a museum recommender system, we take our own project called RFID-Enhanced Museum for Interactive Experience (REMIX) (Karimi *et al.*, 2011d). First, we will describe REMIX and then we will discuss how active learning can be leveraged to improve the quality of its recommendations.

9.1 REMIX Project

Visitors to physical museums are often overwhelmed by the vast amount of information available in the space they are exploring, making it difficult to select personally interesting content. To address this problem, personalized solutions are required in order to provide user-centered interactivity between the visitors and the museum exhibits. Such personalized solutions can be involved to assist visitors during their visit (online case) as well as to enhance their post-museum exploration (offline case), e.g. the interaction that visitors have *after* their visit when they can explore the museum's website and find additional information for the exhibits they are interested in. The advantages of personalized solutions in this form, compared to the involvement of human guides, are their feasibility, efficiency, and lower cost.

Recommender systems are among the most successful personalization technologies, as they have already been incorporated to solve similar problems in e-commerce. The application of recommender systems in the context of museums can be performed in several ways, which may vary from a sophisticated robot to a common mobile device (e.g. smart phone). Developing a recommender system for museums is, however, more challenging than in the case of e-commerce, because in contrast to e-commerce, museums and their exhibits exist in a physical world. Therefore, we need hardware

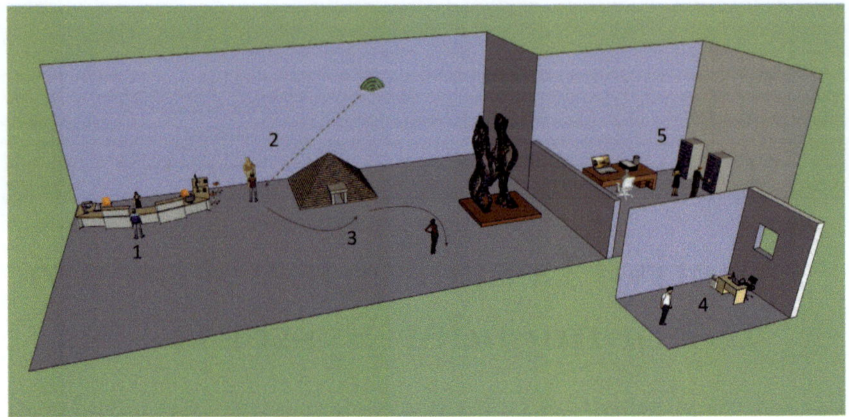

Figure 9.1: REMIX helps visitors to find their favorite exhibits in museums. First, visitors register at a kiosk at the entrance. Then they start their visit. During the visit, REMIX provides recommendations to visitors to view the next exhibit. The picture is from (Karimi *et al.*, 2012b)

technology to provide us with the required infrastructure to observe and model the environment and user activities. Radio-frequency identification (RFID) technology is among the best solutions for this issue, because it is cheap, fast, robust and available anywhere. Finally, algorithms for the generation of recommendations have to take into account the location of exhibits and the physical distance between them.

RFID-Enhanced Museum for Interactive Experience (REMIX) aims to develop a personalization platform for museums based on RFID technology and advanced recommender system algorithms. Our emphasis is on explaining the novel features of the REMIX architecture, which significantly differentiates it from other applications with similar objectives. We also provide details about the challenges faced by recommender system algorithms in this new context. We examine two major cases: i) the online and the ii) offline case. In the online case, visitors are able to get recommendations for exhibits during their visit. Meanwhile, their movements are tracked unobtrusively[1] by RFID sensors placed on the exhibits. In the offline case, after leaving the museum, the visitors can connect to a personalized web-based application, which provides additional information about their actions inside the museum, about the exhibits they have been interested in and recommendations for potentially interesting exhibits that they can see on future visits. Moreover, the tracked information can help the museum's management to understand the behavior and preferences of its visitors and shape evaluation metrics

[1]preserving all aspects of visitors' privacy

for, e.g. the popularity of the exhibits according to their position in the museum in order to reshape policies or design effective campaigns for the future.

The general aim of the REMIX project is the development of a system that advances state-of-the-art research results from the emerging and increasingly affordable field of wireless RFID (Want, 2006) technologies and from the field of recommender systems in the application area of museums. Based on the expected results of REMIX, museums will be able to provide to each visitor with a personalized learning experience and the sense of belonging to the museum's community, which can be extended over multiple visits and between visits via a web application that is developed by the REMIX project. All these factors can significantly help to increase both the number of visitors and the quality of services they are provided with by the museum.

9.2 Related Work

In this section, we provide a brief summary of existing applications for personalized solutions for museums and we detail the innovative aspects of the proposed REMIX system.

The Exploratorium[1] is a hands-on science museum in San Francisco that uses the eXspot system, developed in cooperation with the University of Washington's Computer Science and Engineering Department and Intel Labs Seattle. It is intended to support, record and extend exhibit-based, informal science learning. Its users can bookmark their exhibits of preference, create photographs (using their RFID tags to activate cameras), and access them later via the museum's kiosk or via the internet.

The Museum of Science and Industry in Chicago[2] opened a new 5,000-square foot permanent exhibition called "NetWorld", where visitors can use RFID technology to learn about the internet. First, they design personal avatars, which are stored in the exhibition's network. Then, using their NetPass cards (with embedded RFID chips), the avatars accompany them throughout the exhibition, interacting with them as they learn about bits, packets and bandwidth. With each new exhibit, the network stores visitor ID numbers and displays their avatars to help them through new experiences. To avoid issues of personal data privacy, no personally identifiable information is collected when the cards are issued.

At the Vienna Museum of Technology[3], RFID has been used in an exhibition on the future of virtual reality. Visitors purchase a card at an admission desk, take it to a card-reader terminal and create a personal profile that includes preferred language, favorite color, nicknames and other low-security identifiers. The interaction metaphor represents a digital backpack for collecting multimedia clips. Visitors can take their cards to any number of card-reader terminals in the museum.

[1] `http://www.exploratorium.edu/`
[2] `http://www.msichicago.org/`
[3] `http://www.tmw.at/`

The Museum of Natural History in Aarhus[1] in Denmark uses RFID technology in an exhibit called "Flying," which includes birds tagged with RFID chips. In this exhibit, visitors carry RFID readers and scan the tags attached to the birds. Scanning a bird results in the presentation of associated text, quizzes, audio and video to the visitor.

The Tech Museum in San Jose[2] implemented RFID technologies in the "Genetics: Technology with a Twist" exhibition in 2004. Earlier this year, it launched the "NetP1 Gallery", where visitors create personalized web pages with photographs and images from their visits to the museum, then use their RFID numbers to retrieve the page at anytime on the web.

Similar to the aforementioned existing approaches, the REMIX project involves RFID technology for monitoring visitors. However, it contains several innovative aspects, which differentiate it from existing approaches. These innovative aspects are analyzed as follows:

1. The REMIX information system monitors visitors not only for the purpose of retrieving this information but also to analyze it using data mining technologies. As explained, the transfer of state-of-the-art algorithms from the research field of data mining will allow the museum to better capture user preferences and provide advanced functionalities, such as the recommendation of exhibits for future visits.

2. The information monitored is personalized via a web application that will provide to each visitor with data about the visits and also will encapsulate the data mining results, such as the recommendations.

9.3 The Architecture of REMIX

In this section we describe the overall architecture of the REMIX system.

9.3.1 The RFID Monitoring System

The proposed RFID[3] subsystem in the REMIX architecture monitors the interaction of visitors with exhibits and consists of three main components:

1. **The RFID Reader:** a box carried by visitors. It contains a mote for control and radio connectivity, a low-powered RFID reader with a range of a few centimeters (e.g. 20 cm) and some indicators (e.g. LED) to allow visitors to understand the state of the package.

2. **The RFID Tag:** a small plastic-molded package mounted on exhibits.

[1] `http://www.naturhistoriskmuseum.dk/uk/info/infoUK.htm`

[2] `http://www.tmw.at/`

[3] To get an overview of this technology, please see `http://www.lyngsoesystems.com/RFID/RFID_FAQ.asp`

3. **The wireless network:** RFID readers are connected through a wireless network with a base station. Transmitted information will be sent over mote radio (operating at specific frequency, e.g. 433 MHz). The base station contains a server that maintains the database, where the transmitted information is recorded.

The functionality of the proposed RFID monitoring system is explained as follows: the RFID readers, which are carried by the visitor, continuously monitor their vicinity for the presence of RFID tags. When a visitor approaches an exhibit at a close distance (e.g. 20 cm), the RFID reader reads the RFID tag mounted on the exhibit and sends the ID of the tag to the base station via the wireless network. Along with the ID of the tag, the RFID reader also transmits the ID of the exhibit and the current time. This constitutes the "bookmarking" information that will record the view of the exhibit by the visitor (Figure 9.2).

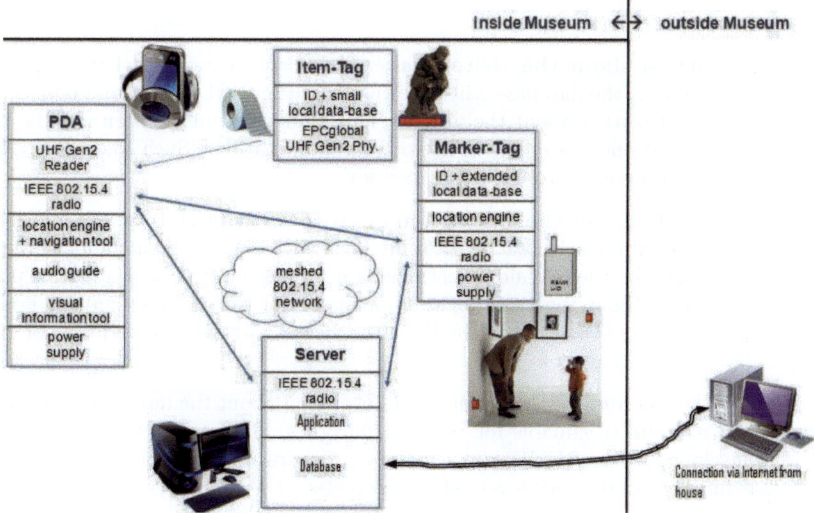

Figure 9.2: The functionality of the REMIX monitoring system

Visitors can obtain their RFID readers at a kiosk at the museum's entrance. They perform a simple registration procedure, by providing some additional low privacy information (like email address or postal code), which increases security in case the RFID reader is lost. They also receive some guidelines about how to use of their RFID readers.

9.3.2 Information System

Information that is going to be transmitted by the RFID monitoring system through the wireless network has to be recorded at the base station. One of the main components of the information system that has been developed by the REMIX project is a database in the base station that contains the following information:

1. **Data about the exhibits:** each exhibit that has a mounted RFID tag is represented in the database. The recorded fields include the ID of the exhibit (unique identifier for each exhibit that will serve as the primary key), the name of the exhibit and additional description, like historical and geographical information pertinent to the exhibit. Moreover, there is additional data for each exhibit in the database, which will be delivered through the web application for post-museum exploration. This information may contain multimedia material, such as photographs or video, hypertext and links to outside articles, such as web encyclopedias.

2. **Data about the visitors:** after each visitor is registered and receives an RFID reader, the database will store the ID of the RFID reader and possibly additional information about the visitor. This additional information may be the visitor's email address or other low-privacy information. Such low-privacy information will serve to protect visitor privacy.

3. **Data about the interaction of visitors with exhibits:** the information about the exhibits that each visitor interacts with during a visit comprises a relationship between the two aforementioned data types, i.e. the data about exhibits and the data about the visitors. More precisely, for each interaction the database stores the ID of the exhibit, the ID of the visitor and the date and time of day that this interaction took place.

The recording of the monitored information about the interactions between visitors and exhibits is valuable for retrieval purposes. Through a web application that was developed by the REMIX project, the visitors are able to retrieve information about the exhibits that they have visited. Nevertheless, the information that is recorded about the interactions between the visitors and the exhibits can serve an additional purpose that is valuable for the museum. Museums can apply data mining techniques over the database contents and analyze the nature of repeat visits and visitor preferences.

Providing recommendations during the current visit (online case) or for future visits (offline case) enriches visitor experience beyond a single visit, increases their satisfaction and provides them with motivation for multiple visits. The information system of the REMIX project performs the analysis of visitor preferences and provides recommendations for exhibits that can be visited on further visits. The functionality of the recommender systems involved and the prediction algorithms for identifying exhibits that have not been visited so far but may interest the visitor on future visits is analyzed in more detail in the following section.

9.4 Developed Web Applications

We developed two web-based applications in the REMIX project. The PDA application (online application) is used by visitors while they are inside museums. And the offline application is used by visitors at home after leaving the museums. The following sections describe an overview of these applications.

9.4.1 PDA Web Application

The PDA application deals with providing recommendations to visitors while they are visiting the museum. At the beginning of the visit, the visitor completes a simple registration and receives an ID. After registration, a PDA is given to the visitor. Visitors cannot use their own PDA because the software already has to be installed on the PDA. The task of this software is to run the localization algorithm and send the results to a server that is already installed at the museum.

Using a web browser, the PDA connects to the web application in the server. In the browser, a map of the museum is shown in which the recommended exhibits are highlighted. While visitors are visiting the museum, they may want to see more information about the exhibits. This information could be text, sound or photos. In this case, they can click on the exhibit in the map to get additional information about exhibits. In addition to the PDA, the visitor carries the RFID reader. The reader reads the RFID tags that are mounted on exhibits and sends the ID of the RFID tag via Bluetooth to the PDA. This application has been implemented with Java. The details of the implementation can be found in (Karimi *et al.*, 2012b).

Figure 9.3 shows the user interface of the PDA application. The visitor's position is indicated by a red circle. The recommended exhibit is highlighted by a red square. All the exhibits that have the same category as the recommended exhibit are highlighted by green squares. Finally, exhibits that have already been viewed by the visitor are highlighted in yellow. Ideally, MF is used for recommendations. However, as we were not able to collect enough data, the initial recommendations were based on a content-based approach. Specifically, the category of exhibits visited by visitors are identified and other exhibits from the same category are recommended to visitors.

In addition to getting recommendations, visitors can click on the exhibits and receive additional information about exhibits, like text and photo. Moreover, visitors can search exhibits on the basis of a lot of different criteria, such as the material of exhibits, the date it was created, the era it belongs to and so on.

9.4.2 Offline Application

When the visitors have left the museum, they can log into a web-based application using their visitor ID. Then a list of the viewed exhibits will appear. Visitors can then click on their favorite exhibit to receive more information, such as video or photos on the exhibit. The application also provides recommendations to the visitor for the next

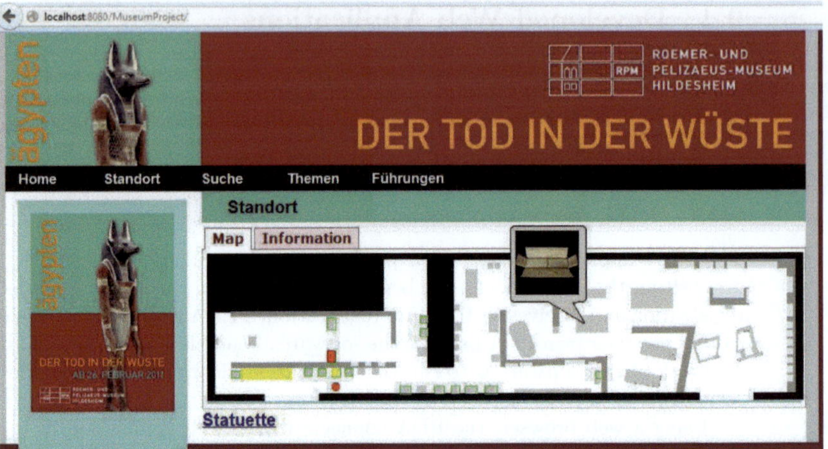

Figure 9.3: The user interface of the PDA application. The visitor's position is indicated by a red circle. The recommended exhibit is highlighted by a red square. All the exhibits that have the same category as the recommended exhibit are highlighted by green squares. Finally, the exhibits that have already been viewed by the visitor are highlighted in yellow.

visit. In this way, the museum will be able to provide to each visitor with a personalized learning experience and the sense of belonging to the museum's community, which can be extended over multiple visits. In addition, visitors are motivated to visit the museum often and each time they can adjust their preferences according to their available time, knowing that they can continue the exploration of the museum in following visits by planning them ahead through the use of recommendations. The proposed web application will offer significant advantages to visitors by offering them further knowledge about the museum's exhibits. It is ideal for pedagogical activities, like a class visiting the museum. As the teacher of the class will not have adequate time during the visit to analyze all the exhibits visited, the proposed web application will allow the teacher in the following days in the class to continue the discussion and exploration of their visit, to assign homework based on the exploitation of additional information, etc.

Figure 9.5 shows the user interface of the offline application. The same functionalities that exist for the PDA application are also available for the offline application, like searching for the exhibits, getting additional information about exhibits and so on. The web application will accommodate the recommendations of exhibits that can be viewed in future visits.

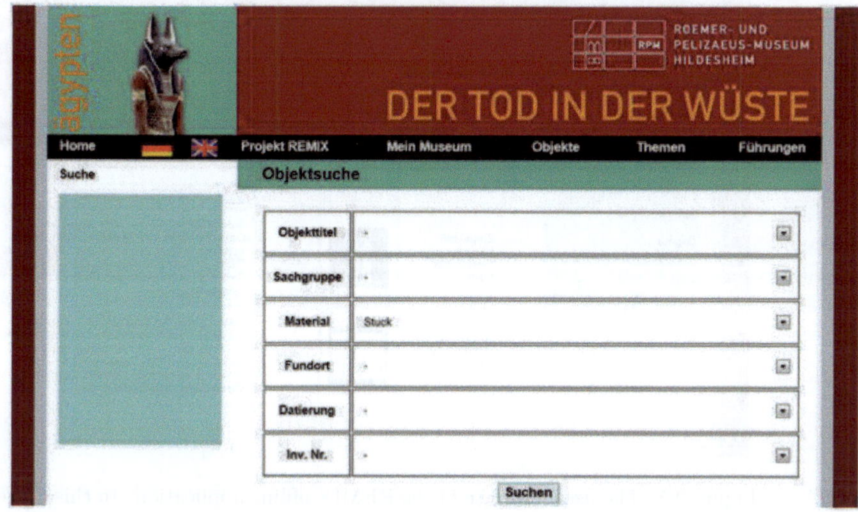

Figure 9.4: visitors can search exhibits based on material, category, title and so on

9.5 Recommendations for New Visitors

As for any other kind of recommender system, museum recommender systems also suffer from the new user problem. Visitors who are visiting a museum for the first time are new users because they have not yet given any feedback to the system. In principle, all active learning methods developed in this thesis can be applied to deal with this problem. However, in this section we propose an active learning method that is specially developed for museum recommender systems.

When new visitors enter a museum, the main challenge for the recommender system is to guide them to the right starting point. As soon as the visitor gets there, the new user problem is almost solved because system can then observe the reaction of the visitor to the exhibits and collect some initial feedback about visitor preferences. Therefore, we define the new user problem in museums as recommending the right starting point. For that, we need to take into account how the exhibits are arranged in the museum.

As a rule, exhibits that are similar to one another are placed in the same area in museums. Similar means they belong to the same category. Therefore, if we find the favorite category of new visitors, we can recommend an exhibit from the corresponding category to them so that they know the best point from which to start their visit.

To find the favorite categories of new users, we need to ask their opinion on different categories before they start their visit. There are two approaches to building such a

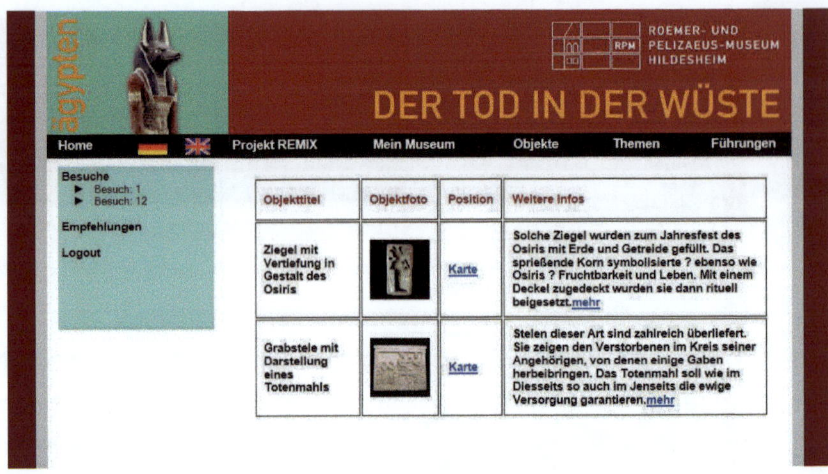

Figure 9.5: The user interface of the REMIX offline application. In this context, offline means it used when visitors have already left the museum.

questionnaire: static and adaptive. In the static approach, the most popular categories are shown to the visitors and they are asked to rate them. In fact, the static approach is batch-mode active learning. In the previous chapters, we have seen some examples of this kind of active learning. This approach would be more suitable for museums with few categories. The more intelligent approach is to build an adaptive questionnaire like decision trees, which were explained in chapter 7. We ask about the first category and then according to the new user's answers, the second category is selected. This approach would be more suitable for museums with many categories.

The preference elicitation process can be done when new visitors are registering in the entrance kiosk to get the RDIF readers. Another possibility is to add this functionality to the offline application. The latter option might be better because new users are willing to answer more questions when they are at home compared to being interviewed in museums.

9.6 Field Trial Evaluation

In order to evaluate the quality of the REMIX, we conducted a field trial test with the participation of all partners and external individuals. The aim of this test was to fix the possible problems. In the end, the participants filled out a survey form and provided their feedback about the system. In total, 10 people took part in the test. Afterwards, some changes were made in the system based on the feedback collected. The changes in the software primarily affected the user interface. The zooming mechanism was improved and tooltips (bubbles) were added to the user interface. On the hardware side, the accuracy of the localization algorithm was improved. Some areas, which were not covered by the wireless network and RFID tags, were also identified.

Some participants were not happy with the initial recommendations. We thought about this problem and came up with the idea proposed in section 9.5. Unfortunately, as the REMIX project has already finished, we were not able to test the proposed idea. We leave this issue as future work.

9.7 Summary and Future Work

In this chapter, we described how active learning can solve the new user problem in museum recommender systems. We relied on our previous project, REMIX, as a museum recommender system. REMIX aims to develop a personalization platform for museums based on RFID technology and advanced recommender system algorithms. Museums invest human and financial resources to improve the learning experience that they offer to their visitors. However, with a large number of permanent exhibits and floor demonstrations, museums offer more choices to the visitors than they can grasp in a single visit. Especially groups of visitors, like school students, tend to carefully observe only a small fraction of the exhibits, as younger visitors usually move fast from one exhibit to another[1]. Therefore, by rushing among the exhibits, visitors cannot fully explore the learning experience provided that the museum has designed for them.

By leveraging RFID technology and through the personalized web application, REMIX allows a museum to intensify the visitor learning experience, to extend it beyond a single visit and to obviate the hurried visitor problem. Moreover, through the analysis of the data collected by the RFID monitoring system, the museum can study the nature of visits and the long-term preferences of the exhibits offered and be in a position to provide better services to its visitors like, for example, recommendations for future visits. With all these means, the museum can increase the number of its visitors, the quality of its services and promote stronger relationships with its visitors, making them feel as members of the museum's community. Therefore, all the aforementioned results are expected to offer financial and cultural benefits to the museum and a better exploitation of its resources. Another benefit is the possibility for additional exploitation of the web personalized application within a business model that can promote advertising information at a regional and national level and e-commerce activities, such as the purchase of souvenirs, books, posters, etc.

Although all active learning methods developed in this thesis can be applied for the new user problem in museum recommender systems, we developed a special active learning method based on the characteristics of a museum. In this method, instead of choosing items, categories are selected for inquiry.

[1]In such cases, the mean time of viewing an exhibit can be less than half a minute.

As future work, we can think of using other recommendation models and then developing active learning methods based on them. There is an essential difference between recommender systems for museum and web-based recommender systems. Web-based recommender systems work in a virtual web environment, but a museum is in the real world. This difference has advantages and disadvantages. In the physical world, there are constraints that do not exist in the virtual world. This issue might put restrictions on the recommendation algorithms. For example, visitors are not willing to visit an exhibit that is far from their current location in the museum. On the other hand, the physical environment provides additional information to enable us to explore new methods that are not applicable to a recommender system working in a virtual environment. For example, in web-based recommender systems, in order to measure the similarity between items, the Euclidean distance is calculated. However, in a museum, it is the physical distance between exhibits that shows how similar the exhibits are. Therefore, there is no need to use other similarity measures. To address this issue, the spatial process technique (Anselin & Syabri, 2006) is a suitable method that has recently been suggested for recommender systems in museums (Bohnert *et al.*, 2009). It would be interesting to develop new active learning methods based on the spacial process and apply it to the museum datasets.

Chapter 10

Conclusion

10.1 Summary

Nowadays, recommender systems have found their place in all domains. They are the main component of many websites, from electronic shops to E-learning applications. Although much progress has been made in developing new recommendation algorithms, their performance drops significantly when it comes to new users. Recommender systems know nothing about new users, so they fail to provide useful recommendations to them. On the other hand, new users are crucial for the profit of recommender systems. Companies spend a lot of money to attract people to their products. It would be a pity if people accepted the companies' invitations and visit the companies' websites and then leave again quickly because they are disappointed with the initial recommendations of the website. Therefore, the cold-start problem is an inevitable challenge for all recommender systems.

In this thesis, we developed several active learning methods for recommender systems. The methods developed have been inspired by the literature on active learning for machine learning. In the recommender system context, new users play the role of the Oracle and provide labels (ratings) to the queries (items). We started with the Aspect Model (AM) as the predictive model for recommender systems and developed active learning for that. According to the learning algorithm of the AM, the most popular items help a lot to improve the new user parameter estimations. Therefore, the proposed method, which is called Most Popular for the Aspect Model (MPAM), chooses the most popular items for the query. The results show that it competes in accuracy with a complicated Bayesian approach, although it is much faster.

After comparing AM to MF and showing that MF outperforms AM, we switched to the MF and proposed four active learning methods for MF. Two methods are based on uncertainty. The first uncertainty measure is based on the learning algorithm of MF. It selects items for which the current predictions are speculated to be very different from the actual rating. The second uncertainty measure relies on the rating matrix to find items for which the predictions are inaccurate. It chooses items for which the predictions are different from the item average predictions based on the training user ratings.

We developed non-myopic active learning for MF. It is based on the exploration-exploitation dilemma. It starts with the exploration by choosing items with small predicted ratings. Such items are expected to lead to maximum change in the new user parameters. In contrast, the exploitation algorithm aims to change the user parameters as little as possible to tune them diligently. This is done by selecting items with a small parameter norm. Finally, we applied the principle of optimal active learning in MF and with some simplifications, we derived a closed-form formula, which approximates the optimal query for MF.

Different from the full Oracle in machine learning, new users are unable to give labels (ratings) to all queries (items). In fact, they are partial Oracle. To address this issue, we changed the setting of the problem in a way that new users are allowed not to rate the queried items. We showed that active learning methods which rely on this constrain do not work at all in the new settings. Then, we developed an active learning that exploits the characteristics of MF to choose items that are likely to be rated by new users.

Decision trees had already been proposed for partial Oracle. Each node represents a step in the sequence of asking queries of new users. Potentially, at each node, there is a branch for all possible answers received from new users, including "Unknown" for the case where new users do not know the queried item. We stick with decision trees and then improved on them from different perspectives. We introduced MF into decision trees. This method is called Factorized Decision Trees(FDT). The FDT constructs the structure of decision trees like the baseline (Golbandi *et al.*, 2011) and then trains an MF model for the last level of decision trees. Furthermore, we extended FDT and developed a new method for initialization in MF. This method benefits from the structure of decision trees. The parameters of MF are initialized with the parameters of MF in the previous level.

We introduced Most Popular Sampling (MPS) to speed up the tree construction. At each node, instead of checking all candidate items, only those that are most popular among the users associated with the node are investigated. It significantly reduces tree construction time without adversely affecting the accuracy. Finally, we upgraded the 3-way split to a 6-way split, meaning each node is split into six nodes, where each child node corresponds to a possible answer provided by new users including "Unknown". As this way of splitting is more-fine grade, it results in better accuracy.

We proposed a new approach for active learning in recommender systems and called it 'Learning Active Learning'. The main idea is to consider past users as (artificial) new users in order to learn the right queries to be asked to new users for active-learning purposes. This constitutes a separate learning problem, in addition to the standard problem of predicting user ratings. We refer to this additional learning problem as 'learning active learning', since we develop a model that will be trained with the ratings of past users in order to predict the right queries to be asked of (actual) new users.

Finally, we showed how active learning can be used for recommender systems in museums. As a museum recommender system, we relied on the REMIX project, which has been developed by us. Museum recommender systems are not able to recommend suitable exhibits to visitors who are visiting a museum for the first time. All the active learning methods developed in this thesis can be exploited to deal with this problem. We also developed a special active learning method for this context. It selects the categories of exhibits and asks the new visitors' opinion on them. Then, an exhibit from the favorite category of new users is recommended to them so that they know where to start their visit.

10.2 Future Directions

Future works have been discussed throughout this thesis at the end of the respective chapters. In addition to those works, we would like to mention three general research directions in this section.

In this thesis we worked on the new user problem. New item and new system are two other important cold-start problems in recommender systems, but were not studied in this thesis. In general, users and items are symmetric, meaning the methods developed for new users can also be applied in new items. However, it would be interesting to validate this hypothesis by running some experiments. Another approach is to take advantage of item attributes. Such attributes do not exist for users. Therefore, we need to develop active learning methods that are special for new items. In chapter 9, we discussed how such attributes can help us to find the right queries for museum recommender systems.

One could argue that there is an essential difference between active learning for new users compared to active learning for new items. New users are not willing to answer many queries, so we have to limit the number of queries. That is why we use active learning. But for a new item, the situation is different. Technically, we can ask all active users to give a rating to a new item. If all of them give the rating, it is perfect. If not, no harm is done. Even if a only small portion of the queries get an answer, it would also be fine. So can we say that there is no need to use active learning for new items? The answer is no!

The point is that there is not only one new item. More new items are added to the system every day . On the other hand, we cannot ask an active user to give ratings to new items every day! The number of queries from active users should be limited, like new users. Otherwise, they won't cooperate with the systems and simply ignore the queries. Therefore, we still need to use active learning for new item problem to select a subset of active users whose opinion on a new item is more helpful for the system. However, the number of the selected users is larger than the number of the selected items for the new user problem. For example, in the case of the Netflix dataset, where there are 480K users, it is feasible to ask, let's say 100 users, to give a rating for a specific new item, while we cannot ask new users to give ratings on 100 items. Note that in the case of the new item problem, there is not an interview step. When a new item is added to the system, after finding the right users to be queried, an email can be sent to them to ask their opinion of the item. Or when they log in to the system, they are asked to rate the new item.

Regarding the new systems, the problem is more difficult than new user or new item because we need to decide on two variables (user and item) simultaneously. In this case, the size of the pool data is equal to all missing ratings in the dataset, which is very large. In the Netfelix dataset, for example, there are around 480K users and 1770 items. Therefore, the total number of possible ratings is around 850M, but only 100M ratings are known and the rest are missing. Moreover, the evaluation protocol would be different for the new system problem. Instead of measuring the test error of new users (new items), the performance of the whole system is evaluated.

Another research direction is to develop active learning methods for other applications besides recommender systems. In recommender systems, the user features and item features are given MF as the predictive model. However, the application of MF is not limited to recommender systems. MF has also been used in other applications, such as computer vision (Heiler & Schnörr, 2006; Shashua & Hazan, 2005) and document clustering (Ma *et al.*, 2010; Xu *et al.*, 2003). These applications probably also face a situation similar to the cold-start problem in recommender systems. In this case, we need to take into account special characteristics of applications to develop active learning methods. For example, in recommender systems we exploit the fact that most of the ratings are large as users usually rate items they like. Such facts may also exist in other applications, which needs to be taken into account.

Finally, while there is a steadily growing, publicly available implementation base for recommendation algorithms, none of the major libraries contains methods for active learning. Can existing recommendation libraries be extended to provide baseline and state-of-the-art methods for active learning for recommender systems that can be used by other researchers to base their experiments on and eventually be used in practice?

Index

References

ABE, N. & MAMITSUKA, H. (1998). Query learning strategies using boosting and bagging. In *Proceedings of the Fifteenth International Conference on Machine Learning*, ICML '98, 1–9, Morgan Kaufmann Publishers Inc., San Francisco, CA, USA. 19

ABRAMSON, Y. & FREUND, Y. (2005). Active learning for visual object recognition. *UCSD tech report.*. 16

ADOMAVICIUS, G. & TUZHILIN, A. (2005). Toward the next generation of recommender systems: A survey of the state-of-the-art and possible extensions. *IEEE Transactions on Knowledge and Data Engineering*, **17**, 734–749. 1

AKIYAMA, T., HACHIYA, H. & SUGIYAMA, M. (2010). Efficient exploration through active learning for value function approximation in reinforcement learning. *Neural Networks*, **23**, 639–648. 17

ANGLUIN, D. (1988). Queries and concept learning. *Mach. Learn.*, **2**, 319–342. 17, 18

ANGLUIN, D. (2001). Queries revisited. In *ALT*, vol. 2225 of *Lecture Notes in Computer Science*, 12–31, Springer. 18

ANSELIN, L. & SYABRI, I. (2006). Geoda: An introduction to spatial data analysis. *Geographical Analysis*, **38**, 5–22. 116

ARGAMON-ENGELSON, S. & DAGAN, I. (1999). Committee-based sample selection for probabilistic classifiers. *Journal of Artificial Intelligence Research*, **11**, 335–360. 18

ATLAS, L., COHN, D., LADNER, R., EL-SHARKAWI, M.A. & MARKS, R.J., II (1990). Training connectionist networks with queries and selective sampling. In *Advances in Neural Information Processing Systems*, 566–573. 18

BARAM, Y., EL-YANIV, R., LUZ, K. & WARMUTH, M. (2004). Online choice of active learning algorithms. *Journal of Machine Learning Research*, **5**, 255–291. 21, 32

BOHNERT, F., SCHMIDT, D.F. & ZUKERMAN, I. (2009). Spatial processes for recommender systems. In *IJCAI*, 2022–2027. 116

BOTTOU, L. (1998). Online learning and stochastic approximations. 82

BOUTILIER, C., ZEMEL, R.S. & MARLIN, B. (2003). Active collaborative filtering. In *Conference on Uncertainty in Artificial Intelligence(UAI)*. 4

BREESE, J.S., HECKERMAN, D. & KADIE, C. (1998). Empirical analysis of predictive algorithms for collaborative filtering. In *Proceedings of the Fourteenth Conference on Uncertainty in Artificial Intelligence*, UAI'98, 43–52. 24

BRINKER, K. (2003). Incorporating diversity in active learning with support vector machines. In *In ICML*. 21

BURKE, R. (2002a). Hybrid recommender systems. *User Modeling and User Adapted Interaction*, **12**, 331–370. 1

BURKE, R. (2002b). Hybrid recommender systems: Survey and experiments. *User Modeling and User-Adapted Interaction*, **12**, 331–370. 2

CHAPELLE, O., SCHÖLKOPF, B. & ZIEN, A., eds. (2006). *Semi-Supervised Learning*. MIT Press, Cambridge, MA. 14

CHEN, T., LI, H., YANG, Q. & YU, Y. (2013). General functional matrix factorization using gradient boosting. In *Proceedings of the 30th International Conference on Machine Learning (ICML-13)*, vol. 28, 436–444, JMLR Workshop and Conference Proceedings. 85

COHN, D., LADNER, R. & WAIBEL, A. (1994). Improving generalization with active learning. In *Machine Learning*, 201–221. 17

COHN, D.A., Z., G. & JORDAN, M. (1995). Active learning with statistical models. In *Advances in Neural Information Processing Systems(NIPS)*. 18, 19, 30, 31, 60, 61, 71

CORTES, C. & VAPNIK, V. (1995). Support-vector networks. In *Machine Learning*, 273–297. 19

CULOTTA, A. & MCCALLUM, A. (2005). Reducing labeling effort for structured prediction tasks. In *Proceedings of the 20th National Conference on Artificial Intelligence - Volume 2*, AAAI'05, 746–751, AAAI Press. 19

DASGUPTA, S. & HSU, D. (2008). Hierarchical sampling for active learning. In *Proceedings of the 25th International Conference on Machine Learning*, ICML '08, 208–215, ACM, New York, NY, USA. 20, 21

DEODHAR, M., GHOSH, J. & SAAR-TSECHANSKY, M. (2009). Active learning for recommender systems with multiple localized models. In *Proc. Fifth Symposium on Statistical Challenges in Electronic Commerce Research*. 4

DESTRERO, A., MOL, C.D., ODONE, F. & VERRI, A. (2007). A regularized approach to feature selection for face detection. 16

ELAHI, M., RICCI, F. & RUBENS, N. (2012). Adapting to natural rating acquisition with combined active learning strategies. In *Proceedings of the 20th International Conference on Foundations of Intelligent Systems*, ISMIS'12, 254–263, Springer-Verlag, Berlin, Heidelberg. 4

ELAHI, M., BRAUNHOFER, M., RICCI, F. & TKALCIC, M. (2013). Personality-based active learning for collaborative filtering recommender systems. In *AI*IA*, vol. 8249 of *Lecture Notes in Computer Science*, 360–371, Springer. 4

ELAHI, M., RICCI, F. & RUBENS, N. (2014). Active learning strategies for rating elicitation in collaborative filtering: A system-wide perspective. *ACM Trans. Intell. Syst. Technol.*, **5**, 13:1–13:33. 4

EPSHTEYN, A., VOGEL, A. & DEJONG, G. (2008). Active reinforcement learning. In *ICML*, vol. 307 of *ACM International Conference Proceeding Series*, 296–303, ACM. 17, 21

FUJII, A., TOKUNAGA, T., INUI, K. & TANAKA, H. (1998). Selective sampling for example-based word sense disambiguation. *Comput. Linguist.*, **24**, 573–597. 18, 19

GANTNER, Z., DRUMOND, L., FREUDENTHALER, C., RENDLE, S. & SCHMIDT-THIEME, L. (2010). Learning attribute-to-feature mappings for cold-start recommendations. In *Proceedings of the 2010 IEEE International Conference on Data Mining*, ICDM '10, 176–185, IEEE Computer Society, Washington, DC, USA. 4

GODBOLE, S., HARPALE, A., SARAWAGI, S. & CHAKRABARTI, S. (2004). Document classification through interactive supervision of document and term labels. In *In PKDD-04*, 185–196. 16

GOLBANDI, N., KOREN, Y. & LEMPEL, R. (2011). Adaptive bootstrapping of recommender systems using decision trees. In *WSDM*, 595–604, ACM. 9, 39, 40, 73, 75, 76, 77, 78, 79, 80, 81, 82, 84, 85, 91, 96, 97, 100, 118

GOLDBERG, D., NICHOLS, D., OKI, B.M. & TERRY, D. (1992). Using collaborative filtering to weave an information tapestry. *Commun. ACM*, **35**, 61–70. 1

GUNAWARDANA, A. & MEEK, C. (2008). Tied boltzmann machines for cold start recommendations. In *Proceedings of the 2008 ACM Conference on Recommender Systems*, RecSys '08, 19–26, ACM, New York, NY, USA. 4

GUO, Y. & GREINER, R. (2007). Optimistic active learning using mutual information. In *Proceedings of the 20th International Joint Conference on Artifical Intelligence*, IJCAI'07, 823–829, Morgan Kaufmann Publishers Inc., San Francisco, CA, USA. 20

Guo, Y. & Schuurmans, D. (2007). Discriminative batch mode active learning. In *NIPS*. 21

Harpale, A.S. & Yang, Y. (2008). Personalized active learning for collaborative filtering. In *Proceedings of the 31st annual international ACM SIGIR conference on Research and development in information retrieval*, 91–98, ACM. 3, 9, 37, 43, 46, 75, 85, 90

Hastie, T., Tibshirani, R. & Friedman, J. (2001). *The Elements of Statistical Learning*. Springer Series in Statistics, Springer New York Inc., New York, NY, USA. 25, 45

Hauptmann, E.G., hao Lin, W., Yan, R., Yang, J. & yu Chen, M. (2006). Extreme video retrieval: joint maximization of human and computer performance. In *In ACM Multimedia*, 385–394, ACM Press. 17

Heiler, M. & Schnörr, C. (2006). Controlling sparseness in non-negative tensor factorization. In *Proceedings of the 9th European Conference on Computer Vision - Volume Part I*, ECCV'06, 56–67, Springer-Verlag, Berlin, Heidelberg. 120

Hofmann, T. (2003). Collaborative filtering via gaussian probabilistic latent semantic analysis. In *Proceedings of the 26th annual international ACM SIGIR conference on Research and development in informaion retrievall*, 259–266, ACM. 3, 24, 46

Hofmann, T. & Puzicha, J. (1999). Latent class models for collaborative filtering. In *International Joint Conference on Artificial Intelligence*, 688–693, Morgan Kaufmann Publishers Inc. 3, 24

Hoi, S.C.H., Jin, R. & Lyu, M.R. (2006a). Large-scale text categorization by batch mode active learning. In *Proceedings of the 15th International Conference on World Wide Web*, WWW '06, 633–642, ACM, New York, NY, USA. 17, 19, 21

Hoi, S.C.H., Jin, R., Zhu, J. & Lyu, M.R. (2006b). Batch mode active learning and its application to medical image classification. In *Proceedings of the 23rd International Conference on Machine Learning*, ICML '06, 417–424, ACM, New York, NY, USA. 21

Huang, Z. (2007). Selectively acquiring ratings for product recommendation. In *Proceedings of the Ninth International Conference on Electronic Commerce*, ICEC '07, 379–388, ACM, New York, NY, USA. 4

Hwa, R. (2004). Sample selection for statistical parsing. *Comput. Linguist.*, **30**, 253–276. 19

Ibbme, J.B., Boger, J. & Boutilier, C. (2005). A decision-theoretic approach to task assistance for persons with dementia. In *In IJCAI*, 1293–1299. 21, 33

JIN, R. & SI, L. (2004). A bayesian approach toward active learning for collaborative filtering. In *Proceedings of the 20th conference on Uncertainty in artificial intelligence*. 3, 9, 10, 36, 37, 43, 44, 46, 47, 50, 68, 75, 85, 90

KARIMI, R., FREUDENTHALER, C., NANOPOULOS, A. & SCHMIDT-THIEME, L. (2011a). Active learning for aspect model in recommender systems. In *CIDM*, 162–167, IEEE. 43

KARIMI, R., FREUDENTHALER, C., NANOPOULOS, A. & SCHMIDT-THIEME, L. (2011b). Towards optimal active learning for matrix factorization in recommender systems. In *23th IEEE International Conference on Tools With Artificial Intelligence (ICTAI)*. 52, 75

KARIMI, R., FREUDENTHALER, C., NANOPOULOS, A. & SCHMIDT-THIEMEE, L. (2011c). Non-myopic active learning for recommender systems based on matrix factorization. In *IEEE Information Reuse and Integration (IRI)*, IEEE. 52, 75

KARIMI, R., NANOPOULOS, A. & SCHMIDT-THIEME, L. (2011d). Rfid-enhanced museum for interactive experience. In *MM4CH*, 192–205, Springer. 1, 4, 7, 105

KARIMI, R., FREUDENTHALER, C., NANOPOULOS, A. & SCHMIDT-THIEMEE, L. (2012a). Exploiting the characteristics of matrix factorization for active learning in recommender systems. In *RecSys*, 317–320. 52, 75

KARIMI, R., WANG, H. & GEORGI, B. (2012b). Remix final reprt. 106, 111

KARIMI, R., WISTUBA, M., NANOPOULOS, A. & SCHMIDT-THIEME, L. (2013). Factorized decision trees for active learning in recommender systems. In *ICTAI*, 404–411, IEEE. 73

KING, R.D., WHELAN, K.E., JONES, F.M., REISER, P.G.K., BRYANT, C.H., MUGGLETON, S.H., KELL, D.B. & OLIVER, S.G. (2004). Functional genomic hypothesis generation and experimentation by a robot scientist. *Nature*, **427**, 247–252. 18

KIRKPATRICK, S., GELATT, C.D. & VECCHI, M.P. (1983). Optimization by simulated annealing. *Science*, **220**, 671–680. 20

KOHRS, A. & MERIALDO, B. (2001). Improving collaborative filtering for new users by smart object selection. In *International Conference on Media Features (ICMF)*. 33, 35

KONSTAN, J.A., MILLER, B.N., MALTZ, D., HERLOCKER, J.L., GORDON, L.R. & RIEDL, J. (1997a). GroupLens: Applying collaborative filtering to usenet news. *Communications of the ACM*, **40**, 77–87. 1, 2

KONSTAN, J.A., MILLER, B.N., MALTZ, D., HERLOCKER, J.L., GORDON, L.R., RIEDL, J. & VOLUME, H. (1997b). Grouplens: Applying collaborative filtering to usenet news. *Communications of the ACM*, **40**, 77–87. 33

KOREN, Y. (2007). How useful is a lower rmse? `http://www.netflixprize.com/community/viewtopic.php?id=828/`, accessed: 15-04-2013. 12, 85

KOREN, Y. (2008). Factorization meets the neighborhood: a multifaceted collaborative filtering model. In *Proceedings of the 14th ACM SIGKDD international conference on Knowledge discovery and data mining*, KDD '08, 426–434, ACM. 3, 26, 54

KOREN, Y., BELL, R. & VOLINSKY, C. (2009). Matrix factorization techniques for recommender systems. *Computer*, **42**, 30–37. 2, 25, 26, 27, 55

KRAUSE, A. & GUESTRIN, C. (2007). Nonmyopic active learning of gaussian processes: An exploration-exploitation approach. In *Proceedings of the 24th International Conference on Machine Learning*, ICML '07, 449–456, ACM, New York, NY, USA. 18

KRISHNAMURTHY, V. (2002). Algorithms for optimal scheduling and management of hidden markov model sensors. *IEEE Transactions on Signal Processing*, **50**, 1382–1397. 18

LAFFERTY, J.D., MCCALLUM, A. & PEREIRA, F.C.N. (2001). Conditional random fields: Probabilistic models for segmenting and labeling sequence data. In *Proceedings of the Eighteenth International Conference on Machine Learning*, ICML '01, 282–289, Morgan Kaufmann Publishers Inc., San Francisco, CA, USA. 19

LANDWEHR, N., HALL, M. & FRANK, E. (2005). Logistic model trees. *Mach. Learn.*, **59**, 161–205. 76

LANG, K.J. & BAUM, E.B. (1992). Query learning can work poorly when a human oracle is used. 18

LARSEN, D.R. & SPECKMAN, P.L. (2004). Multivariate Regression Trees for Analysis of Abundance Data. *Biometrics*, **60**, 543–549. 76

LESKOVEC, J., KRAUSE, A., GUESTRIN, C., FALOUTSOS, C., VANBRIESEN, J. & GLANCE, N. (2007). Cost-effective outbreak detection in networks. In *Proceedings of the 13th ACM SIGKDD International Conference on Knowledge Discovery and Data Mining*, KDD '07, 420–429, ACM, New York, NY, USA. 18

LEWIS, D.D. & CATLETT, J. (1994). Heterogeneous uncertainty sampling for supervised learning. In *In Proceedings of the 11th International Conference on Machine Learning (ICML*, 148–156, Morgan Kaufmann. 19

LEWIS, D.D. & GALE, W.A. (1994). A sequential algorithm for training text classifiers. In *Proceedings of the 17th Annual International ACM SIGIR Conference on Research and Development in Information Retrieval*, SIGIR '94, 3–12, Springer-Verlag New York, Inc., New York, NY, USA. 17, 19

LI, S.Z. & ZHANG, Z. (2004). Floatboost learning and statistical face detection. *IEEE TRANSACTIONS ON PATTERN ANALYSIS AND MACHINE INTELLIGENCE*, **26**, 2004. 16

LINDENBAUM, M., MARKOVITCH, S. & RUSAKOV, D. (2004). Selective sampling for nearest neighbor classifiers. *Mach. Learn.*, **54**, 125–152. 19

LIU, Y. (2004). Active learning with support vector machine applied to gene expression data for cancer classification. *J. Chemistry Information and Computer Science*, **44**, 1936–1941. 17

LOPES, M., MELO, F.S. & MONTESANO, L. (2009). Active learning for reward estimation in inverse reinforcement learning. In *European Conference on Machine Learning (ECML/PKDD)*, Bled, Slovenia. 17, 21

MA, H., ZHAO, W., TAN, Q. & SHI, Z. (2010). Orthogonal nonnegative matrix tri-factorization for semi-supervised document co-clustering. In *Proceedings of the 14th Pacific-Asia Conference on Advances in Knowledge Discovery and Data Mining - Volume Part II*, PAKDD'10, 189–200, Springer-Verlag, Berlin, Heidelberg. 120

MAIRAL, J., BACH, F., PONCE, J. & SAPIRO, G. (2010). Online learning for matrix factorization and sparse coding. *J. Mach. Learn. Res.*, **11**, 19–60. 82

MELVILLE, P. & MOONEY, R.J. (2004). Diverse ensembles for active learning. In *Proceedings of the Twenty-first International Conference on Machine Learning*, ICML '04, 74–, ACM, New York, NY, USA. 19

MOSKOVITCH, R., NISSIM, N., STOPEL, D., FEHER, C., ENGLERT, R. & ELOVICI, Y. (2007). Improving the detection of unknown computer worms activity using active learning. In *KI*, 489–493. 20

NEWEY, W.K. & MCFADDEN, D. (1994). Large sample estimation and hypothesis testing. In *International Conference on Information Visualisation*. 62

NGUYEN, T. & SMEULDERS, A. (2004). Active learning using pre-clustering. In *International Conference on Machine Learning (ICML)*. 20, 21, 32

NICHOLAS, R. & MCCALLUM, A. (2001). Toward optimal active learning through monte carlo estimation of error reduction. In *International Conference on Machine Learning (ICML)*. 17, 20, 31, 32, 75

OSUGI, T., KUN, D. & SCOTT, S. (2005). Balancing exploration and exploitation: A new algorithm for active machine learning. In *IEEE International Conference on Data Mining (ICDM)*. 32, 34, 57

PARK, S.T. & CHU, W. (2009). Pairwise preference regression for cold-start recommendation. In *Proceedings of the Third ACM Conference on Recommender Systems*, RecSys '09, 21–28, ACM, New York, NY, USA. 4

PENNOCK, D.M., HORVITZ, E., LAWRENCE, S. & GILES, C.L. (2000). Collaborative filtering by personality diagnosis: A hybrid memory and model-based approach. In *Proceedings of the 16th Conference on Uncertainty in Artificial Intelligence*, UAI '00, 473–480, Morgan Kaufmann Publishers Inc., San Francisco, CA, USA. 2

POUPART, P. (March 2009). Non-myopic active learning: A reinforcement learning approach. In *Google Talk*. 21, 33

RASHID, A.M., ALBERT, I., COSLEY, D., LAM, S.K., MCNEE, S.M., KONSTAN, J.A. & RIEDL, J. (2002). Getting to know you: Learning new user preferences in recommender systems. In *Proceedings of the International Conference on Intelligent User Interfaces*, 127–134, ACM Press. 9, 35

RASHID, A.M., KARYPIS, G. & RIEDL, J. (2008). Learning preferences of new users in recommender systems: an information theoretic approach. *SIGKDD Explor. Newsl.*, **10**, 90–100. 37, 38, 39, 96

RENDLE, S. & SCHMIDT-THIEME, L. (2008). Online-updating regularized kernel matrix factorization models for large-scale recommender systems. In *ACM Conference on Recommender Systems (RecSys)*, 251–258, ACM. 27, 44, 45, 54, 57, 58, 62, 79

RESNICK, P. & VARIAN, H.R. (1997). Recommender systems. *Commun. ACM*, **40**, 56–58. 1

RICCARDI, G. & HAKKANI-TR, D. (2003). Active and unsupervised learning for automatic speech recognition. 17

RICCARDI, G. & HAKKANI-TR, D. (2005). Active learning: theory and applications to automatic speech recognition. *IEEE Transactions on Speech and Audio Processing*, **13**, 504–511. 17

RISH, I. & TESAURO, G. (2008). Active collaborative prediction with maximum margin matrix factorization. In *ISAIM*. 4

RODRÍGUEZ, J.J., GARCÍA-OSORIO, C., MAUDES, J. & DÍEZ-PASTOR, J.F. (2010). An experimental study on ensembles of functional trees. In *Proceedings of the 9th International Conference on Multiple Classifier Systems*, MCS'10, 64–73, Springer-Verlag, Berlin, Heidelberg. 76

RUBENS, N. & SUGIYAMA, M. (2007). Influence-based collaborative active learning. In *Proceedings of the 2007 ACM Conference on Recommender Systems*, RecSys '07, 145–148, ACM, New York, NY, USA. 4

SAFOURY, L. & SALAH, A. (2013). Exploiting user demographic attributes for solving cold-start problem in recommender system. *Lecture Notes on Software Engineering*, **1**, 303–307. 4

SALAKHUTDINOV, R. & MNIH, A. (2008). Probabilistic matrix factorization. In *Advances in Neural Information Processing Systems*, vol. 20. 51

SCHEIN, A.I., POPESCUL, A., UNGAR, L.H. & PENNOCK, D.M. (2002). Methods and metrics for cold-start recommendations. In *Proceedings of the 25th Annual International ACM SIGIR Conference on Research and Development in Information Retrieval*, SIGIR '02, 253–260, ACM, New York, NY, USA. 2

SCHERVISH, M.J. (1995). *Theory of Statistics*. Springer-Verlag, New York, NY. 19, 21

SCHOHN, G. & COHN, D. (2000). Less is more: Active learning with support vector machines. In *International Conference on Machine Learning (ICML)*. 52, 61

SEGAL, M.R. (1992). Tree-structured Methods for Longitudinal Data. *Journal of the American Statistical Association*, **87**, 407–418. 76

SETTLES, B. (2010). Active learning literature survey. Tech. rep. 17, 18

SETTLES, B. & CRAVEN, M. (2008). An analysis of active learning strategies for sequence labeling tasks. In *Proceedings of the Conference on Empirical Methods in Natural Language Processing*, EMNLP '08, 1070–1079, Association for Computational Linguistics, Stroudsburg, PA, USA. 17, 19, 20, 21

SETTLES, B., CRAVEN, M. & RAY, S. (2008). Multiple-instance active learning. In *In Advances in Neural Information Processing Systems (NIPS*, 1289–1296, MIT Press. 20

SEUNG, H.S., OPPER, M. & SOMPOLINSKY, H. (1992). Query by committee. In *Proceedings of the Fifth Annual Workshop on Computational Learning Theory*, COLT '92, 287–294, ACM, New York, NY, USA. 19

SHANNON, C.E. (1948). A mathematical theory of communication. *Bell system technical journal*, **27**. 19

SHASHUA, A. & HAZAN, T. (2005). Non-negative tensor factorization with applications to statistics and computer vision. In *Proceedings of the 22Nd International Conference on Machine Learning*, ICML '05, 792–799, ACM, New York, NY, USA. 120

SUGIYAMA, M. (2006). Active learning in approximately linear regression based on conditional expectation of generalization error. *J. Mach. Learn. Res.*, **7**, 141–166. 31

SUGIYAMA, M. & RUBENS, N. (2008). Active learning with model selection in linear regression. 31

SUTHERLAND, D.J., PÓCZOS, B. & SCHNEIDER, J. (2013). Active learning and search on low-rank matrices. In *Proceedings of the 19th ACM SIGKDD International Conference on Knowledge Discovery and Data Mining*, KDD '13, 212–220, ACM, New York, NY, USA. 4

SUTTON, R.S. & BARTO, A.G. (1998a). *Introduction to Reinforcement Learning*. MIT Press, Cambridge, MA, USA, 1st edn. 32

SUTTON, R.S. & BARTO, A.G. (1998b). *Reinforcement Learning: An Introduction*. MIT Press. 17

TEYTAUD, O., GELLY, S. & MARY, J. (2007). Active learning in regression, with application to stochastic dynamic programming. In *ICINCO-ICSO*, 198–205, INSTICC Press. 21

THOMPSON, C.A., CALIFF, M.E. & MOONEY, R.J. (1999). Active learning for natural language parsing and information extraction. In *Proceedings of the Sixteenth International Conference on Machine Learning (ICML-99)*, 406–414, Bled, Slovenia. 17

TONG, S. & CHANG, E. (2001). Support vector machine active learning for image retrieval. In *Proceedings of the Ninth ACM International Conference on Multimedia*, MULTIMEDIA '01, 107–118, ACM, New York, NY, USA. 17

TONG, S. & KOLLER, D. (2000a). Active learning for parameter estimation in bayesian networks. In *Advances in Neural Information Processing Systems(NIPS)*. 17, 36

TONG, S. & KOLLER, D. (2000b). Support vector machine active learning with application sto text classification. In *ICML*, 999–1006. 19

TONG, S. & KOLLER, D. (2002). Support vector machine active learning with applications to text classification. *J. Mach. Learn. Res.*, **2**, 45–66. 16, 32

TUR, G., HAKKANI-TÜR, D. & SCHAPIRE, R.E. (2005). Combining active and semi-supervised learning for spoken language understanding. *Speech Communication*, **45**, 171–186. 17

VAPNIK, V.N. & CHERVONENKIS, A.Y. (1971). On the uniform convergence of relative frequencies of events to their probabilities. *Theory of Probability and its Applications*, **16**, 264–280. 20

VIOLA, P. & JONES, M. (2001). Robust real-time object detection. In *International Journal of Computer Vision*. 16

WANT, R. (2006). An introduction to rfid technology. *IEEE Pervasive Computing*, **5**, 25–33. 107

WARMUTH, M.K., RTSCH, G., MATHIESON, M., LIAO, J. & LEMMEN, C. (2001). Active learning in the drug discovery process. In *NIPS*, 1449–1456, MIT Press. 17

XU, W., LIU, X. & GONG, Y. (2003). Document clustering based on non-negative matrix factorization. In *Proceedings of the 26th Annual International ACM SIGIR Conference on Research and Development in Informaion Retrieval*, SIGIR '03, 267–273, ACM, New York, NY, USA. 120

XU, Z., AKELLA, R. & ZHANG, Y. (2007). Incorporating diversity and density in active learning for relevance feedback. In *Proceedings of the 29th European Conference on IR Research*, ECIR'07, 246–257, Springer-Verlag, Berlin, Heidelberg. 20, 21

YAN, R., YANG, J. & HAUPTMANN, A. (2003). Automatically labeling video data using multi-class active learning. In *Proceedings of the Ninth IEEE International Conference on Computer Vision - Volume 2*, ICCV '03, 516–, IEEE Computer Society, Washington, DC, USA. 17

YANG, B., SUN, J.T., WANG, T. & CHEN, Z. (2009). Effective multi-label active learning for text classification. In *Proceedings of the 15th ACM SIGKDD International Conference on Knowledge Discovery and Data Mining*, KDD '09, 917–926, ACM, New York, NY, USA. 16

YU, D., VARADARAJAN, B., DENG, L. & ACERO, A. (2010). Active learning and semi-supervised learning for speech recognition: A unified framework using the global entropy reduction maximization criterion. *Comput. Speech Lang.*, **24**, 433–444. 17

YU, H. (2005). Svm selective sampling for ranking with application to data retrieval. In *Proceedings of the Eleventh ACM SIGKDD International Conference on Knowledge Discovery in Data Mining*, KDD '05, 354–363, ACM, New York, NY, USA. 18

ZHANG, C. & CHEN, T. (2002). An active learning framework for content based information retrieval. *IEEE TRANS. ON MULTIMEDIA, SPECIAL ISSUE ON MULTIMEDIA DATABASE*, **4**, 260–268. 17

ZHANG, C. & ZHANG, Z. (2010). A survey of recent advances in face detection. 16

ZHANG, H. (1998). Classification Trees for Multiple Binary Responses. *Journal of the American Statistical Association*, **93**, 180–193. 76

ZHANG, L., MENG, X., CHEN, J., XIONG, S.C. & DUAN, K. (2009). Alleviating cold-start problem by using implicit feedback. In *ADMA*, vol. 5678 of *Lecture Notes in Computer Science*, 763–771, Springer. 4, 28

ZHANG, T. & OLES, F.J. (2000). A probability analysis on the value of unlabeled data for classification problems. In *Proc. 17th International Conf. on Machine Learning*, 1191–1198. 19

ZHOU, K., YANG, S.H. & ZHA, H. (2011). Functional matrix factorizations for cold-start recommendation. In *Proceedings of the 34th international ACM SIGIR conference on Research and development in Information Retrieval*, SIGIR '11, 315–324, ACM. 9, 40, 41, 79, 85

ZHU, X., LAFFERTY, J. & GHAHRAMANI, Z. (2003). Combining active learning and semi-supervised learning using gaussian fields and harmonic functions. In *ICML 2003 workshop on The Continuum from Labeled to Unlabeled Data in Machine Learning and Data Mining*, 58–65. 20

ZIGORIS, P. (2006). Bayesian adaptive user profiling with explicit & implicit feedback. In *In Conference on Information and Knowledge Mangement*, 397, ACM Press. 4, 28